KERBER ART

SOMNAMBUL

TYPLT

Schöpferische Lust an der Malerei
Christoph Tannert

Ob Lubomír Typlt die Welt um ihn herum mit wachsendem Befremden betrachtet, ist nicht gewiss. Man wüsste gern, ob er sich Sorgen macht. Die Welt verändert sich ständig – nicht aber die großen Fragen, die Menschen bewegen. An die Bilder aus den Kriegen und von den ökologischen Katastrophen haben wir uns gewöhnt. Aber die Besorgnis ist verschwunden. Wir brauchen neue, zeitgemäße Erzählungen, die der Absurdität unseres Endzeitalters entsprechen. Typlt lässt keinen Zweifel daran, dass sich das Schicksal des Planeten jetzt entscheidet. Nach fast dreißig „postideologischen" Jahren sind die Ängste aus der Zeit des Kalten Krieges abstrakt fern. Aber an Verwerfungen der Seele ist die Gegenwart reich, vielleicht sogar reicher als alle hypochondrischen Befürchtungen einer Psychiatrie, die an ihrem Menschenbild krankt. Um die Krisen und Jammertäler, durch die wir heutzutage irren, zu deuten, als erschreckend bis existenzbedrohend, braucht es Metaphern. Und zwar neue. Denn derzeit sieht es so aus, als seien die alten Slogans – Klimawandel, Massentierhaltung, MeToo – ausgelutscht, unbrauchbar, verdächtig.

Typlt, mit zupackenden Bildern auf semantischer Leuchtspur, hilft uns auf die Sprünge. Sein bengalisch flackernder Farbreigen kommt zur rechten Zeit. Mit Gänsehaut produzierenden Szenarien malt Typlt an gegen das allgemeine Augenschließen. Ein bewusst herber, geräuschvoller, ungefälliger Touch ist nicht zu übersehen. Es geht um bildnerisches Reibungspotenzial. Man kann diese atmosphärische Note als Resultat deutscher Wurstigkeit betrachten (denn Typlt hat in Düsseldorf u. a. bei Lüpertz und Penck studiert). Vielleicht hat der Künstler seine Stoffe aber auch unbewusst aus den Albträumen des tschechischen Surrealisten Jan Švankmajer gehäkelt. Mag das Spiel mit den Augäpfeln [1] zwar formschlüssig, aber von der Erzählung her brutal anmuten, der an den Haarschöpfen reißende Wind [2] ist nicht weniger unerbittlich. Er weht aus der Undurchschaubarkeit und hat damit eine enge Beziehung zum Unheimlichen.

Obwohl Typlt die pathetische Geste in der Kunst fremd ist, gibt es dennoch einen Grundzug von Pathos im Werk: Es ist die kategorische Absage an das Vergessen, der Widerstand, Spuren der Verletzungen unserer Tageauszublenden. Amdeutlichsten tritt dieses Druckpotenzial in den Texten des Künstlers hervor, die er 2005 für die tschechische Band WWW geschrieben hat, die wegen ihres Progressive Industrial Sounds in unserem Nachbarland einen gewissen Kultstatus genießt. Typlt scheint eine ähnlich skeptische Grundhaltung zu besitzen, wie man sie bereits aus der großartigen tschechischen Undergroundliteratur der kommunistischen Ära her kennt. Was er schreibt, markiert eine Frustration, die aus Erfahrungen der Sinnentleertheit des Daseins resultiert. So heißt es z. B. in einem Song von WWW: „Ich fühle mich wie eine Zahl in der Zahlenreihe. Ich bin klein. Geteilt. Und für immer minus." [3] Und an anderer Stelle: „Ich sehne mich nach Vergeltung. Für eine lange Zeit." [4] Diese Dualität zwischen Entmutigung und Gegenangriff heizt Typlt bisweilen bis zum Siedepunkt auf. Und dann nimmt er wieder die Kälte und verbrennt sie. Er weigert sich, das Handtuch zu werfen. So entstehen neuartige Bilder, die Energieträger sind, die durch Eiszeiten führen. Selten hat jemand Figürlichkeit so dringlich als Ganzkörperwahrnehmung inszeniert.

Wenn man sich einlässt auf die spezielle Figürlichkeit, die Typlt mit Bildkraft zum Leben erweckt, wird man sein Vergnügen haben, weil er ganz in unserer Zeit steht und zugleich immer wieder darüber hinausweist. Die schöpferische Lust des Umgangs mit der menschlichen Figur hat er auf eine wirklich eigenständige Bahn geführt. Er nimmt Aspekte des Figurativen zum Ausgangspunkt, um sie dann verrätselt wiederzugeben als ein malerisches Erlebnis. Einzelgänger und Einzelgängerinnen, Sekundanten und Sekundantinnen, Opportunisten und Gelehrte treten auf als Hofschranzen in Kinderkörpern. Typlt legt figurative Fährten in Neonlicht und in Violett – als der Farbe der Macht, aber auch der Leidenschaft, des Unmoralischen, der Heilung sowie des Todes.

Etwas Erwartbares abzuschnurren entspricht nicht dem Ansatz dieses Künstlers, vielmehr liebt er es, sich vom Dekorativen und Sentimentalen fernzuhalten und aparte Seitenwege einzuschlagen. Natürlich ist man gewarnt, weil dieser Ausnahmekünstler mit Haut und Haaren Tscheche ist. Aber er ist auch ein Künstler, der ganz in der Malerei mit ihren eigenen Gesetzen und damit im Überzeitlichen steht. Seine Heimat liegt in der Präsenz der Farbe.

Anmerkungen

[1] Zum Beispiel in den Bildern „Einzelgängerinnen", „Einzelgänger in Violett" und „Zu Hause".

[2] Zum Beispiel in den Bildern „Somnambul", „Zieh mir an den Haaren", „Japanerinnen im Wind", „Abendstern", „Sekundantinnen", „Duell" und „Der Wind wirft keine Schatten".

[3] Je mi jako číslici v číselné řadě. Jsem krácen. Dělen a věčně v mínusu. Zitat aus dem Titel „Pramen ústní vody" der Band WWW auf dem Album „Neurobeat" (2006).

[4] Dlouho toužím po odvetě. Už dlouho. Zitat aus dem Titel „Štěstí" der Band WWW auf dem Album „Neurobeat" (2006).

Creative Pleasure in Painting
Christoph Tannert

It is not certain whether Lubomír Typlt looks at the world around him with a growing sense of alienation. One would like to know if he is worried. The world may be constantly changing – but not so the big questions that mankind has been contemplating through the ages. We have grown used to images of wars and ecological disasters. But we are no longer really concerned. We need new, contemporary narratives that reflect the absurdity of our apocalyptic age. Typlt leaves no doubt that the fate of the planet is being decided now. After nearly thirty 'post-ideological' years, the anguish of the Cold War period seems like a far and abstract memory. Yet the present is rich in twistings of the soul, maybe even richer than all the hypochondriacal fears of psychiatry, stuck in its flawed idea of humankind. Metaphors are needed if we want to grasp the crises and vales of tears through which we are stumbling as terrifying or existential in nature. New metaphors, that is. Because right now, the old slogans – climate change, factory farming, MeToo – seem stale, dysfunctional, suspicious.

Typlt helps us by lighting the way along a semantic path of gripping images. His brazen, fiery palette of colours comes at the right time. With scenes that are certain to give viewers goosebumps, he paints against general indifference. His painting evidences a deliberately harsh, noisy, unaccommodating touch. It revolves around the potential of images to create friction. This atmospheric note can be seen as a reaction to German apathy (Typlt studied with Lüpertz and Penck in Düsseldorf, among others). Maybe the artist's work is woven from the nightmares of the Czech surrealist Jan Švankmajer. While his play with eyeballs may seem formally coherent,[1] though brutal in terms of narrative, the wind tearing at the hair is equally relentless.[2] Originating from an area that remains inscrutable, it entertains a close relationship with the uncanny.

Although Typlt's art is a stranger to pathetic gestures, it is nevertheless underpinned by pathos – that is, the categorical rejection of oblivion, the refusal to hide the traces of the injuries of our day. This potential to resist is most evident in the texts he wrote in 2005 for the Czech band WWW, whose progressive industrial sound has earned it a kind of cult status with our neighbours. Typlt would appear to perpetuate a sceptical attitude familiar from the great Czech underground literature of the Communist era. His writing bears witness to a frustration that results from the repeated experience of the meaninglessness of existence. One of his songs for WWW states: 'I feel like a number in a series of numbers. I am small. Divided. And forever minus.'[3] Another says: 'I long for retribution. For a long time.'[4] Occasionally, this duality between despair and reprisal reaches a boiling point in Typlt's work. And then he takes on the cold again and burns it. He refuses to throw in the towel, creating novel images that act like carriers of energy leading through ice ages. Few artists have staged figurativeness so persistently as a holistic physical perception.

Provided one agrees to engage with this singular figurativeness that Typlt brings to life with bold pictorial vigour, one is rewarded with great pleasure because he is so completely of our time and yet ceaselessly points beyond it. He has channelled the creative pleasure in exploring the human figure into a genuinely unique approach, taking certain aspects of figuration as a starting point, which he then reproduces in riddled form as a painterly experience. Loners, opportunists and scholars appear as servile courtiers in children's bodies. Typlt lays figurative tracks in neon light and purple – the colour of power but also of passion, immorality, healing and death.

To simply spool off something that is expected would not be consistent with Typlt's approach, as he steers clear from decoration and sentimentality, preferring to walk the less familiar path instead. Of course, viewers are warned because this exceptional artist is as Czech as it gets. But he is also an artist who is entirely steeped in painting and its own laws, and therefore in timelessness. His home lies in the presence of colour.

[1] See e.g. the paintings *Einzelgängerinnen* (Loners), *Einzelgänger in Violett* (Loner in Purple) and *Zu Hause* (At Home).

[2] See e.g. the paintings *Somnambul* (Somnambulistic), *Zieh mir an den Haaren* (Pull my Hair), *Japanerinnen im Wind* (Japanese Women in the Wind), *Abendstern* (Evening Star), *Sekundantinnen* (Seconds to the Duel), *Duell* (Duel) and *Der Wind wirft keine Schatten* (Wind Does Not Cast Shadows).

[3] 'Je mi jako číslici v číselé řadě. Jsem krácen. Dělen a věčně v mínusu.' Quoted from the song 'Pramen ústní vody' on the album *Neurobeat* (2006) by WWW.

[4] 'Dlouho toužím po odvetě. Už dlouho.' Quoted from the song 'Štěstí' on the album *Neurobeat* (2006) by WWW.

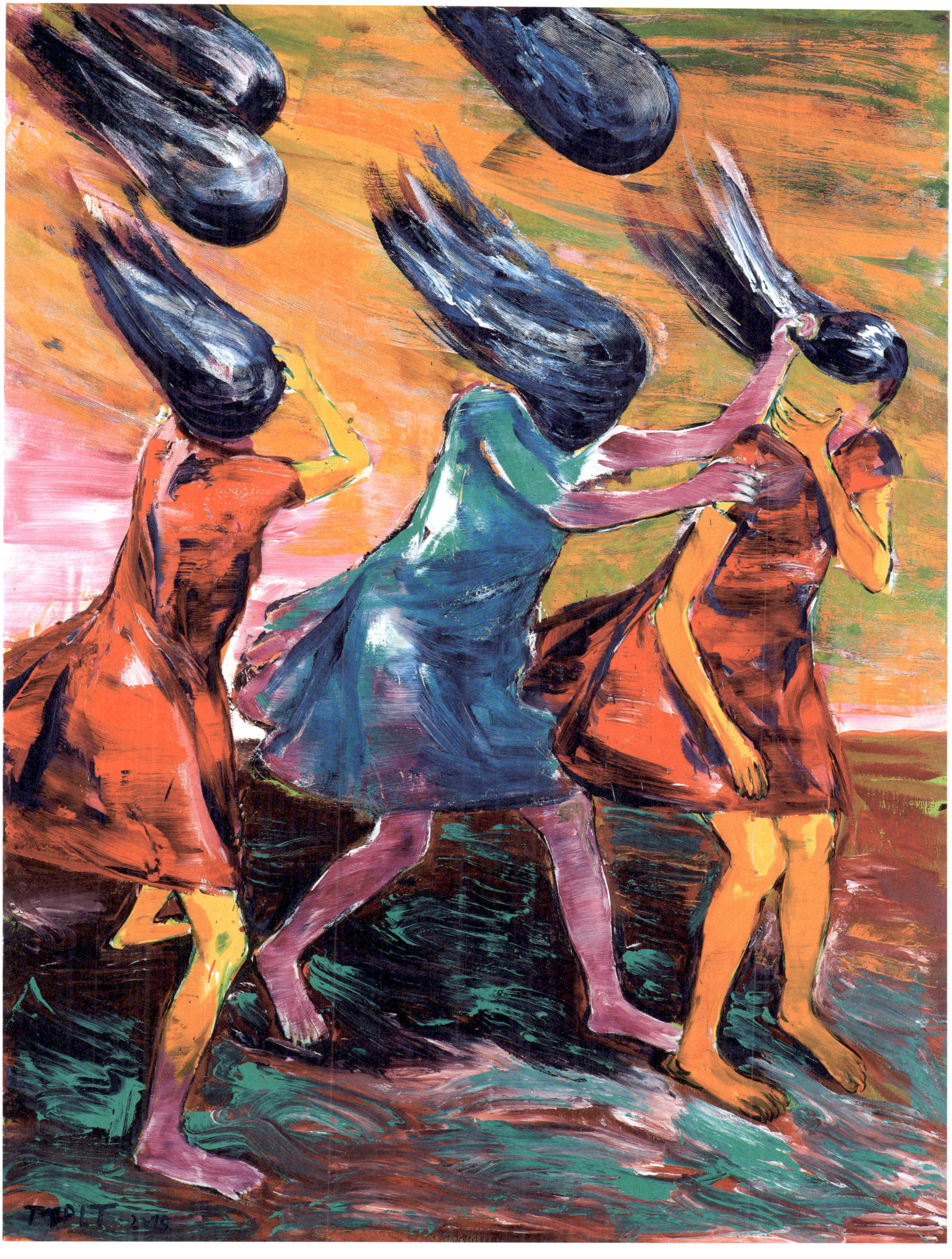

Zieh mir an den Haaren / Pull my Hair
2015, Öl auf Leinwand, 240 × 180 cm

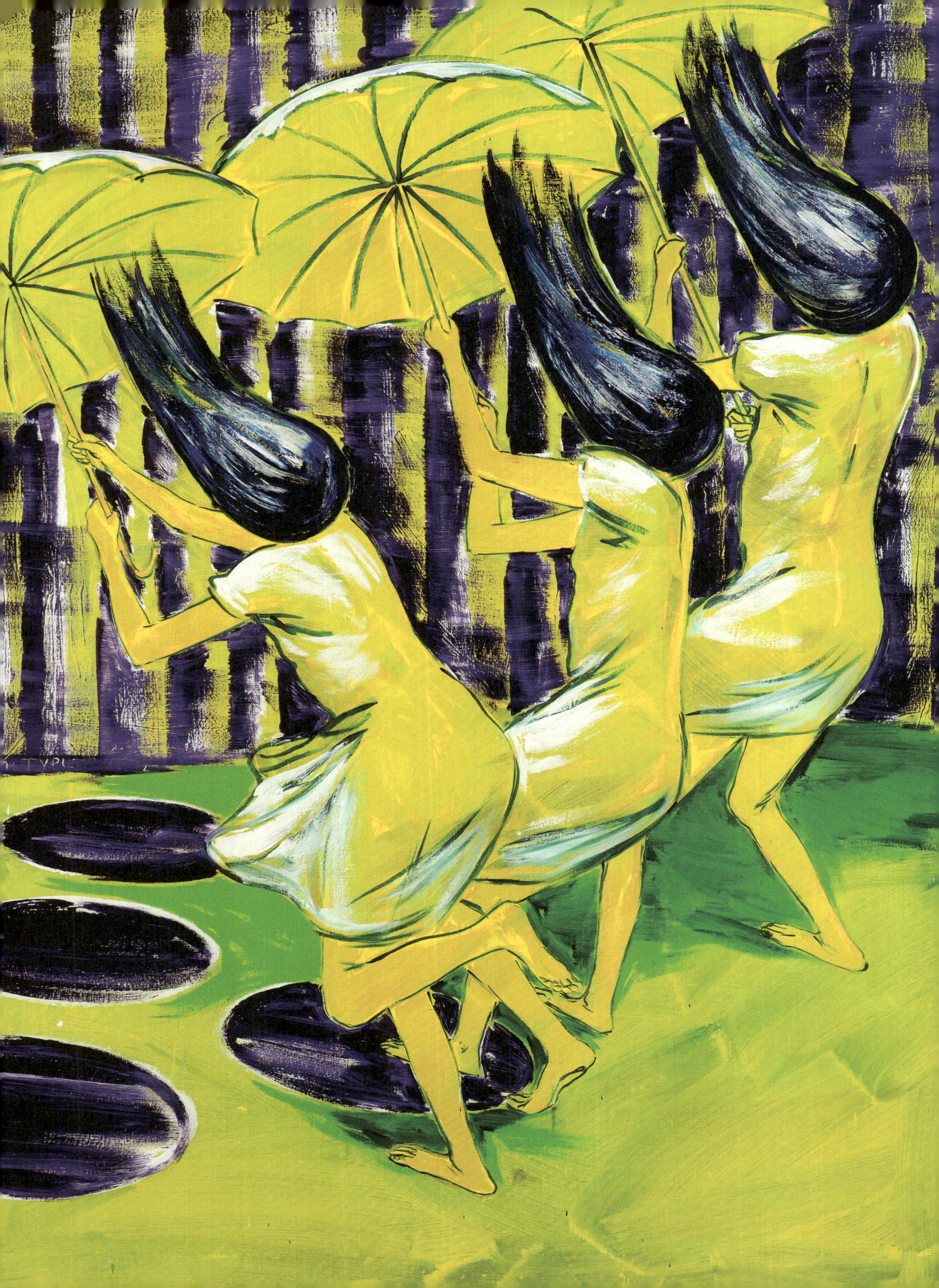

Japanerinnen im Wind / Japanese Women in the Wind
2019, Öl auf Leinwand, 240 × 180 cm

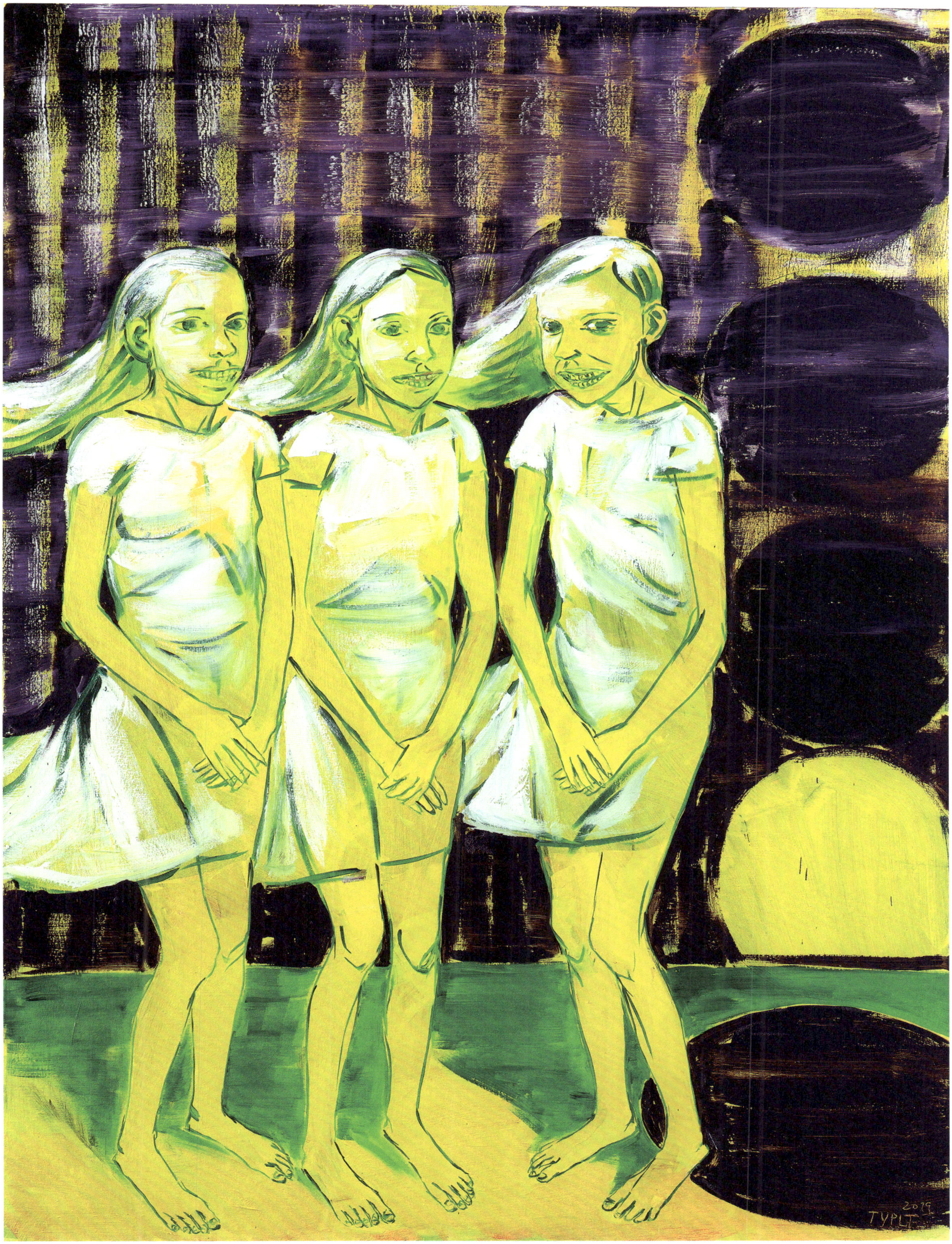

Violette Sonne / Purple Sun
2019, Öl auf Leinwand, 240 × 180 cm

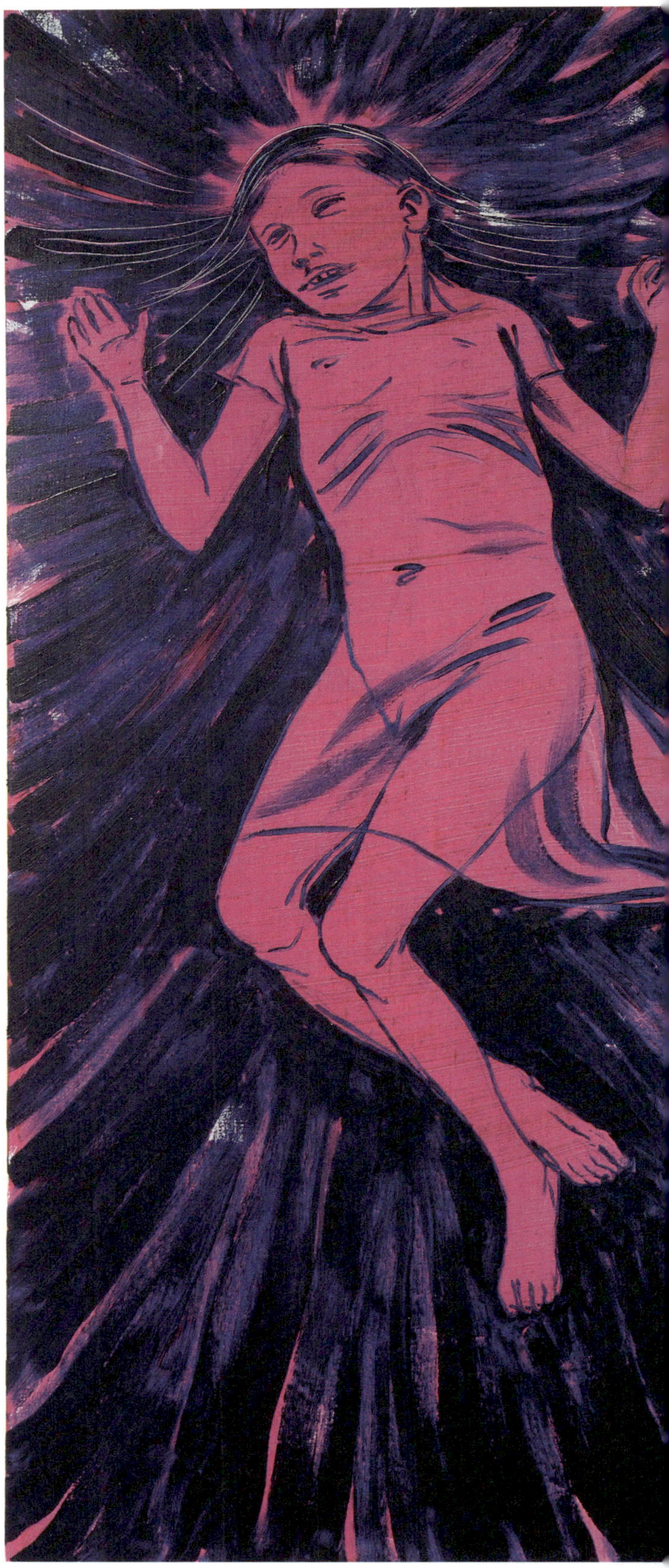

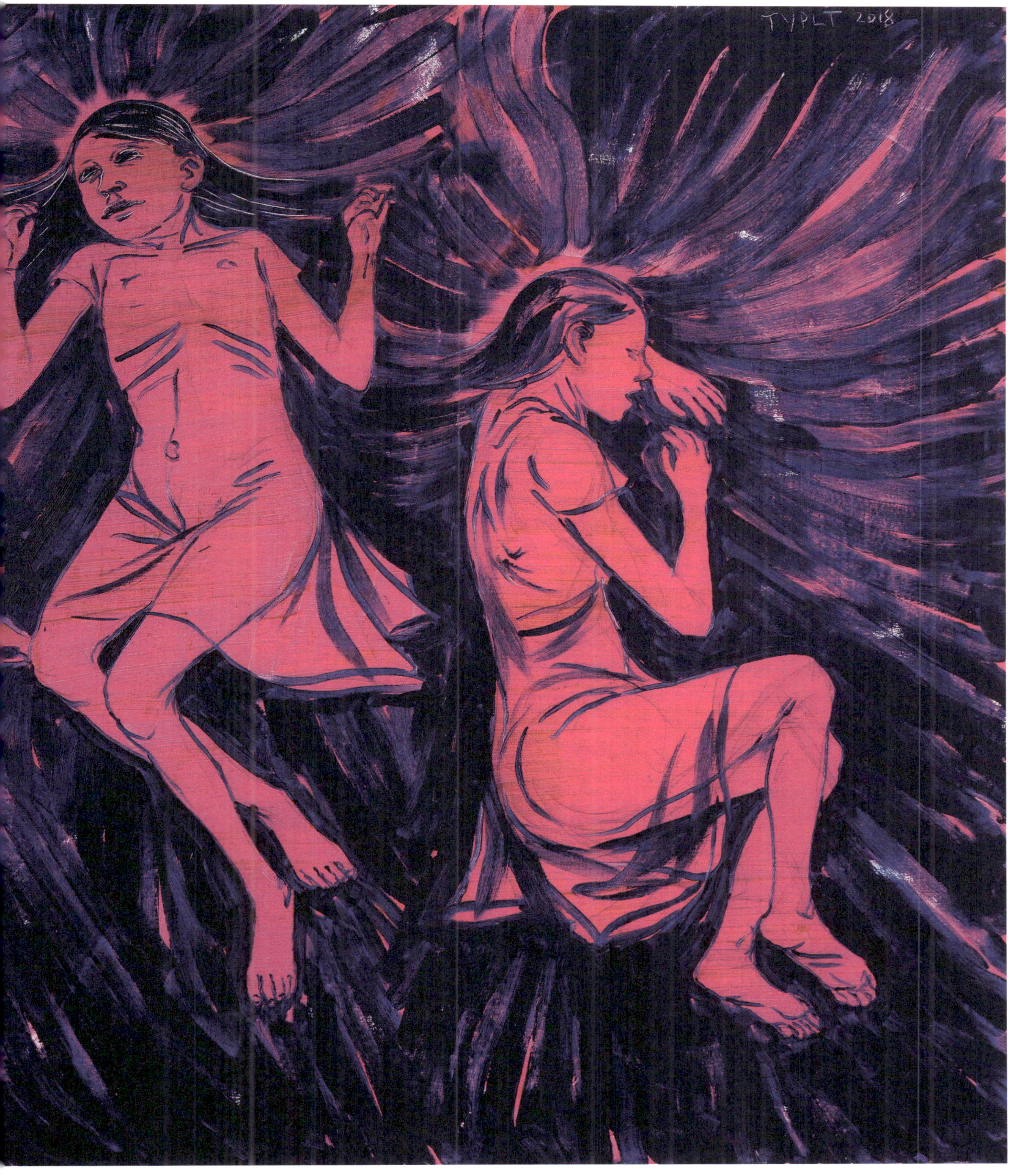

Sonne im Vollmond / Sun in the Full Moon
2018, Öl auf Leinwand, 200 × 260 cm

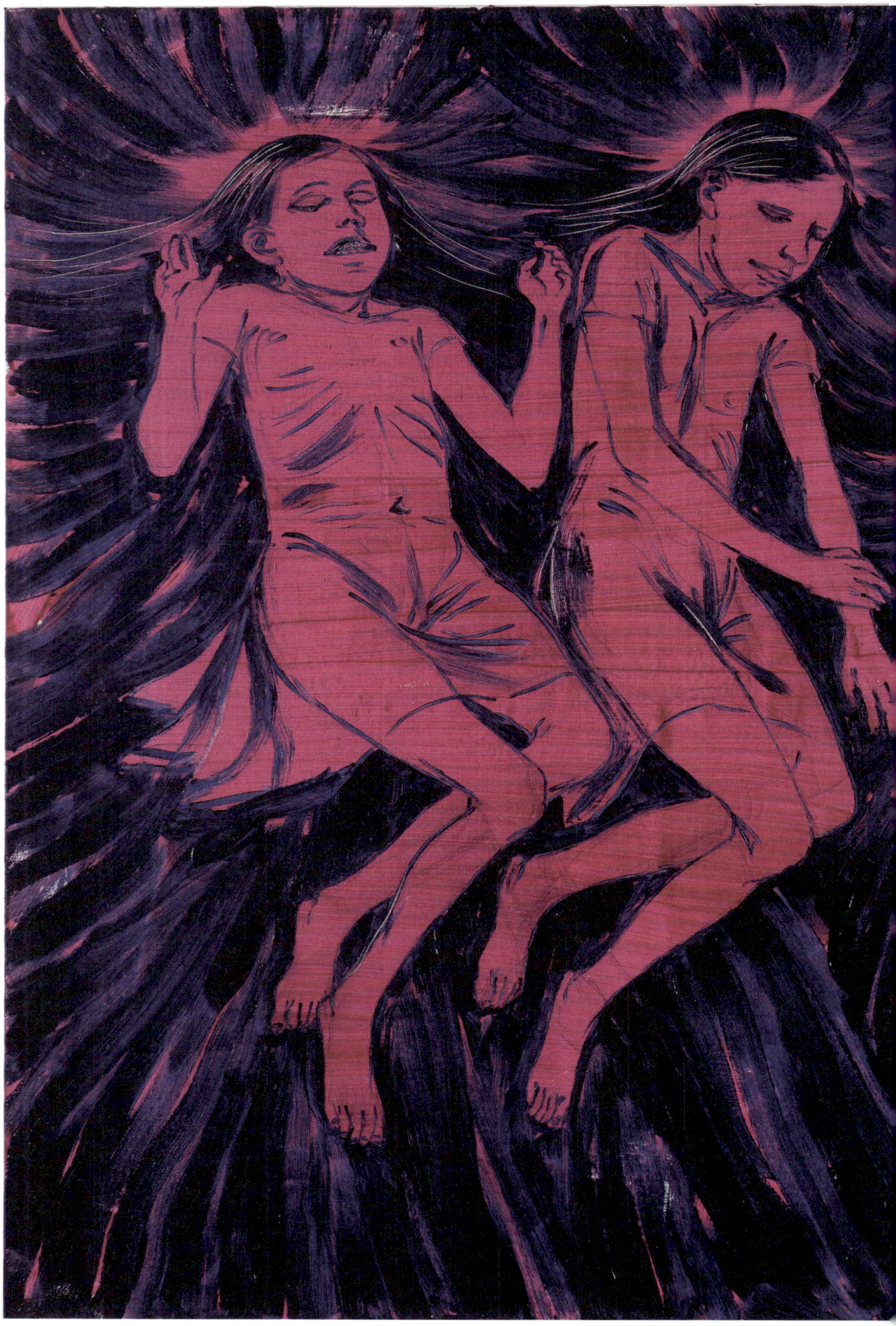

Bring mir das Phosphor aller Streichholzköpfe / Bring All the Match-Heads You Can Find
2018, Öl auf Leinwand, 200 × 260 cm

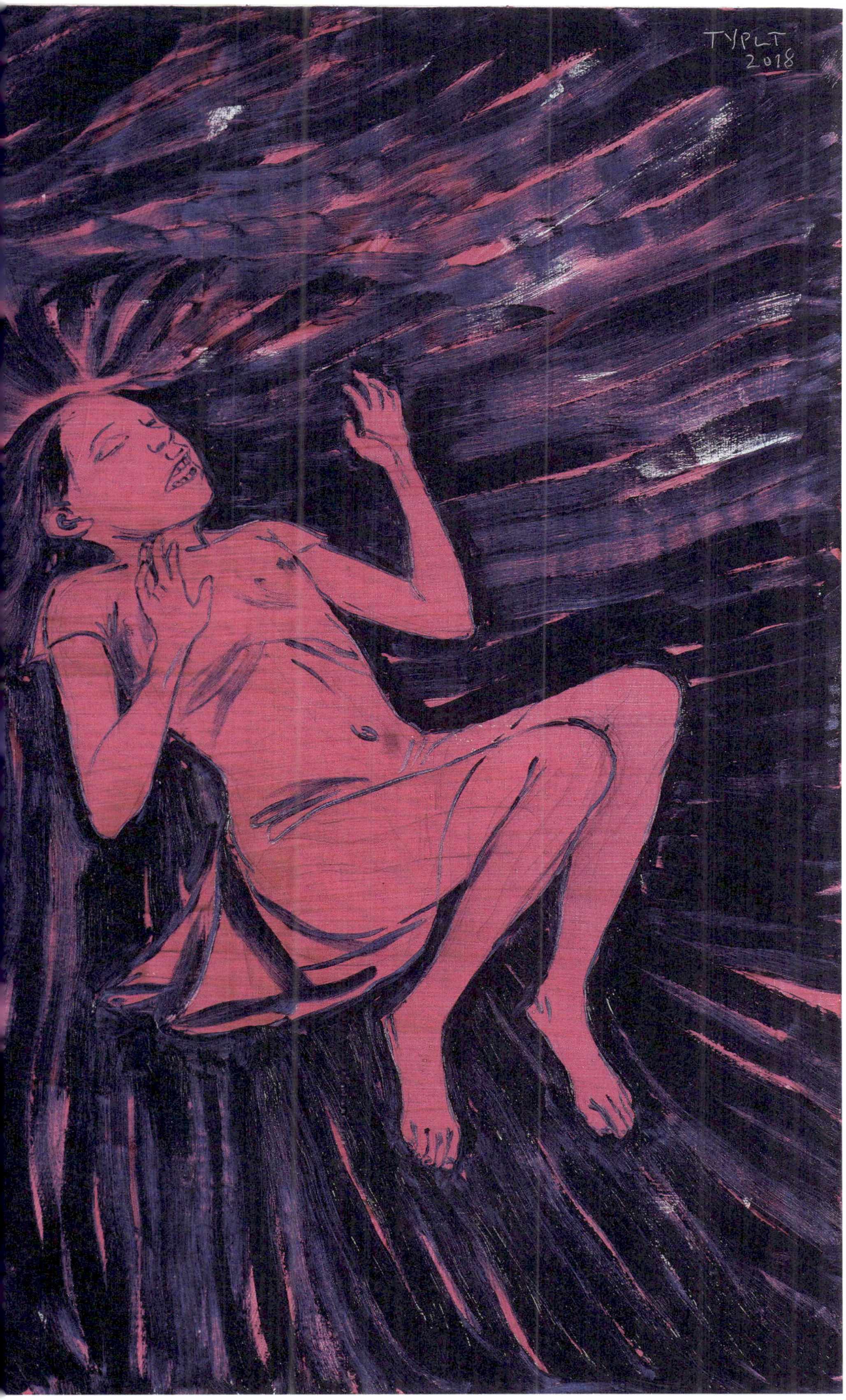
TYPLT
2018

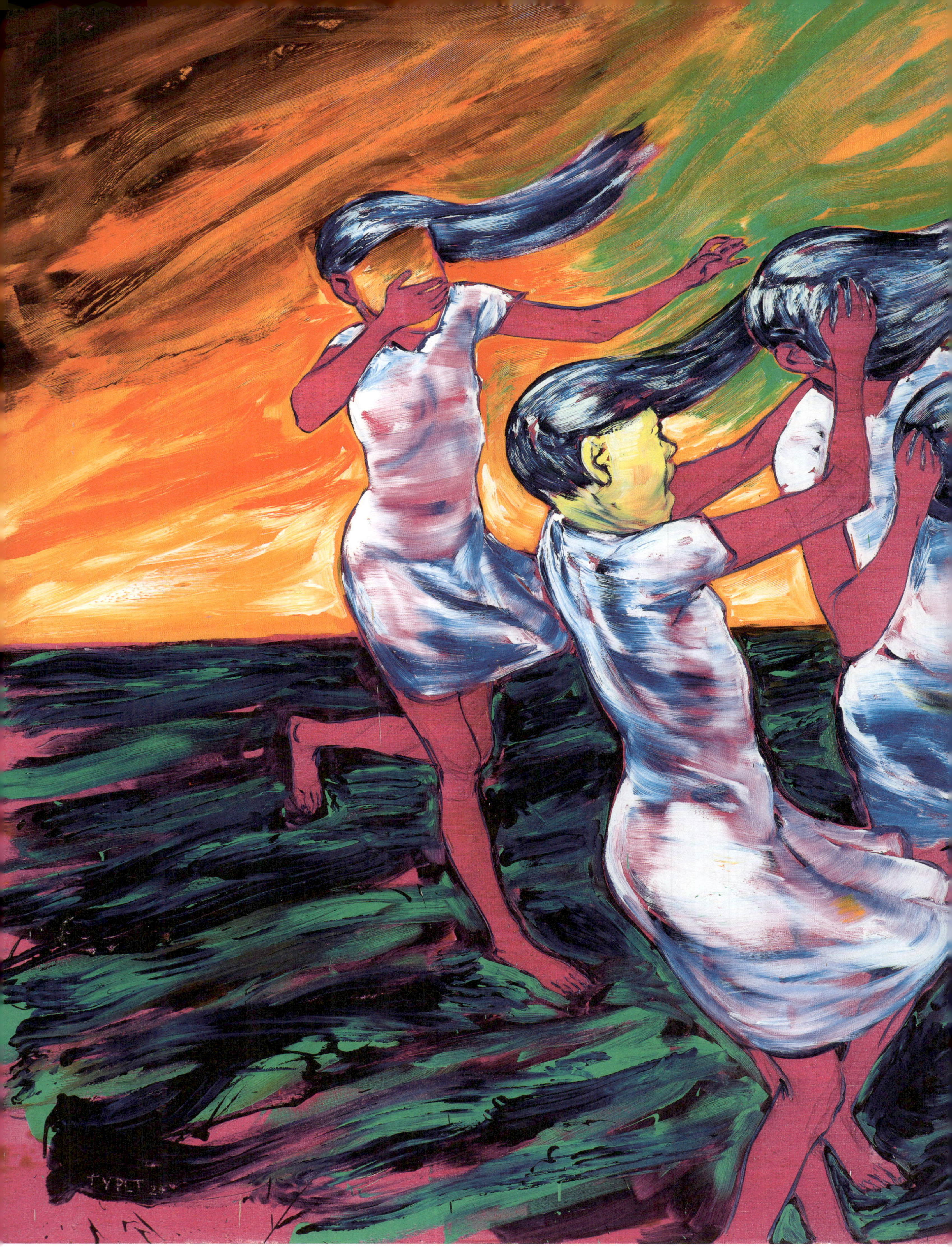

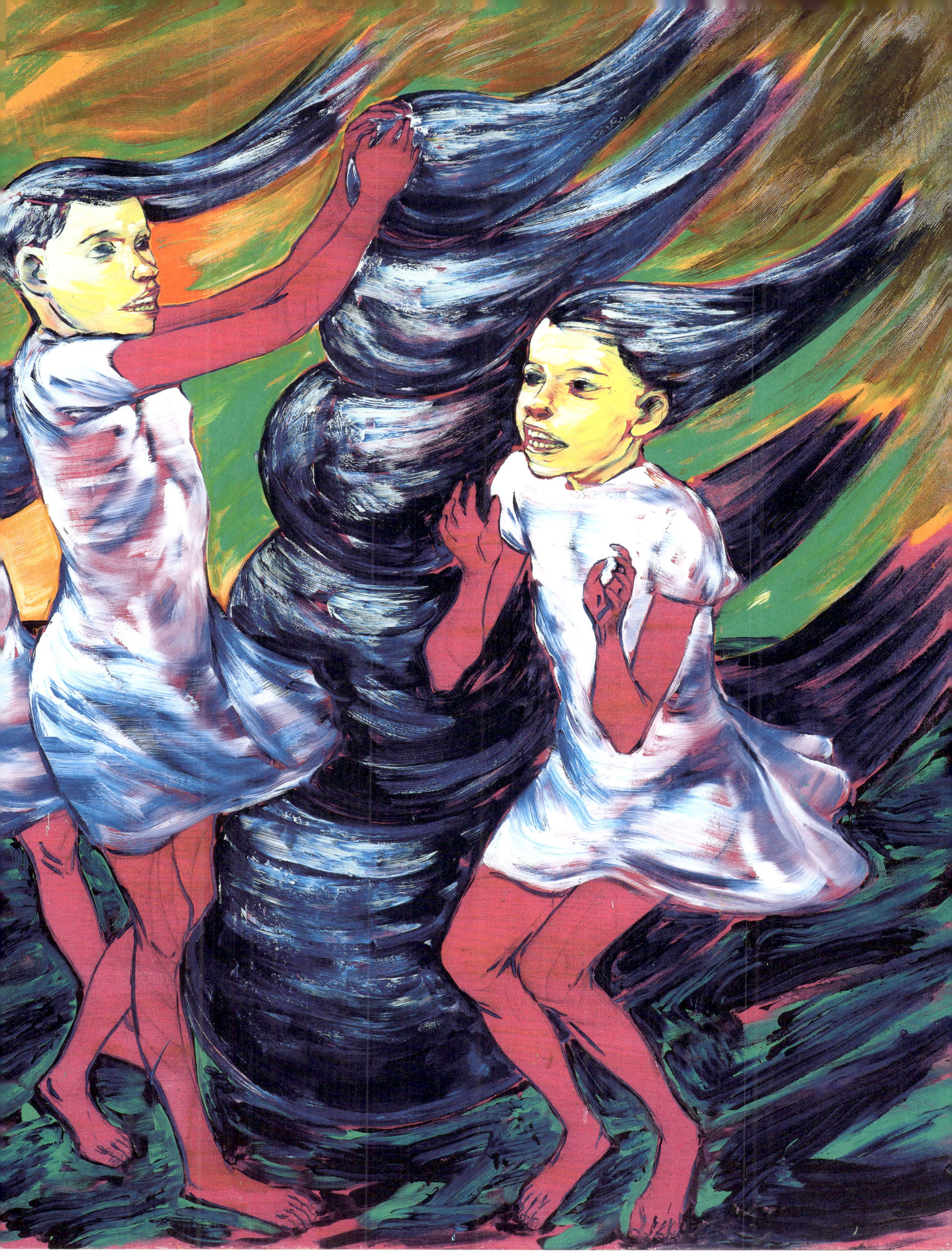

Der Wind wirft keinen Schatten / Wind Casts No Shadow
2020, Öl auf Leinwand, 240 × 360 cm (zweiteilig)

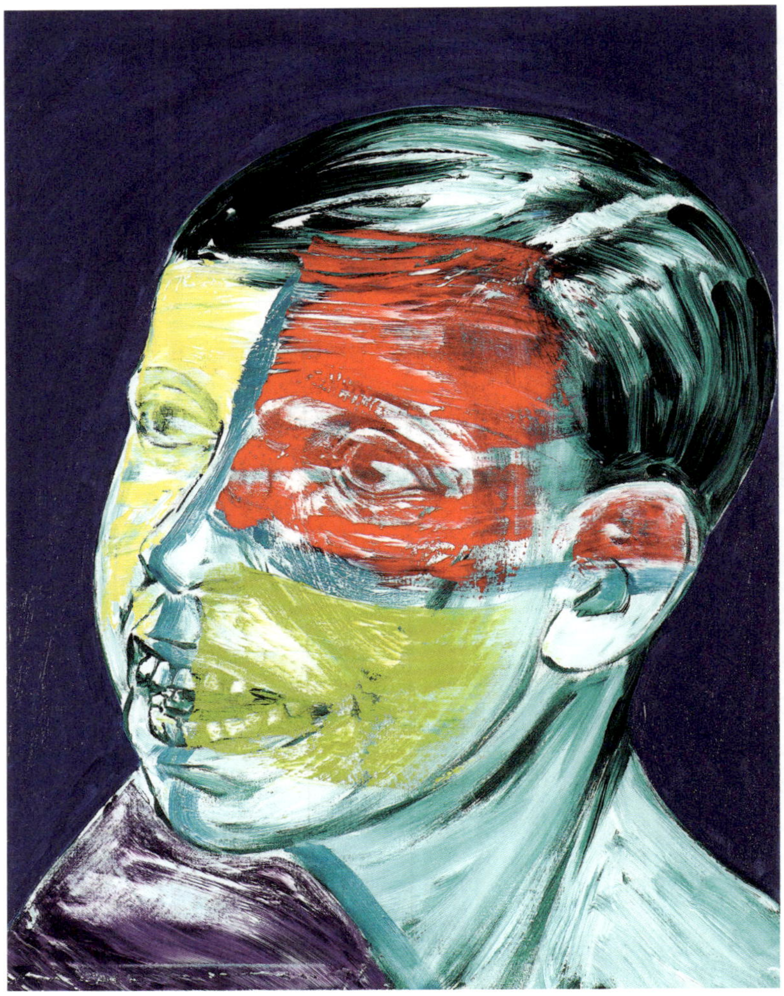

Illusionist / Illusionist
2020, Öl auf Leinwand, 130 × 100 cm

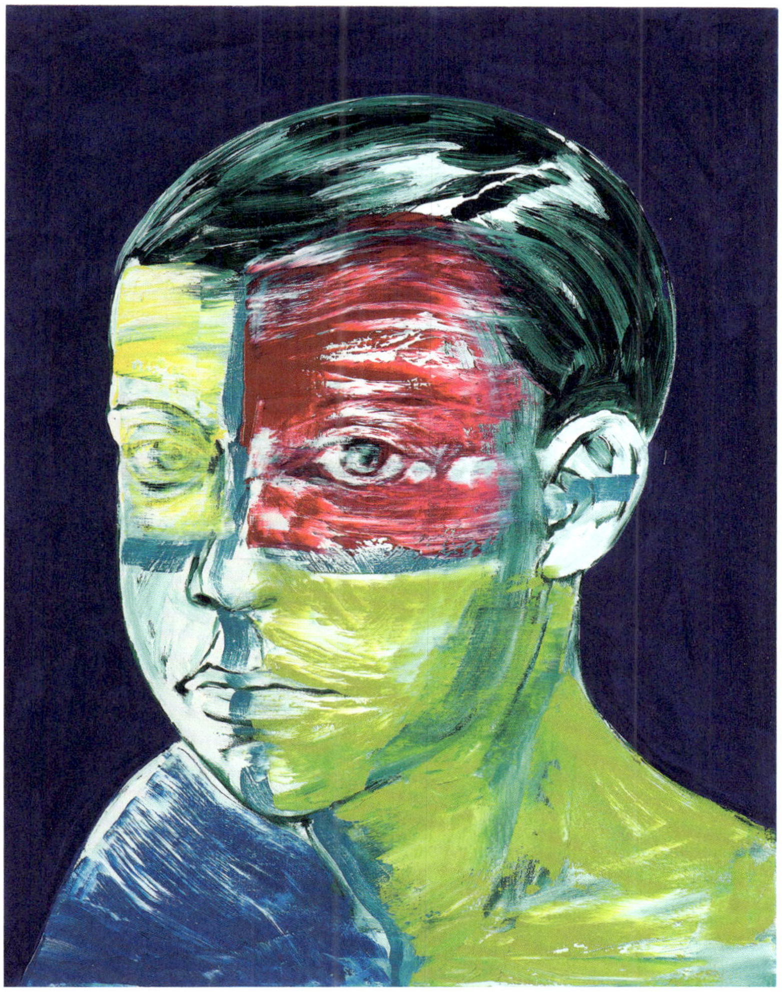

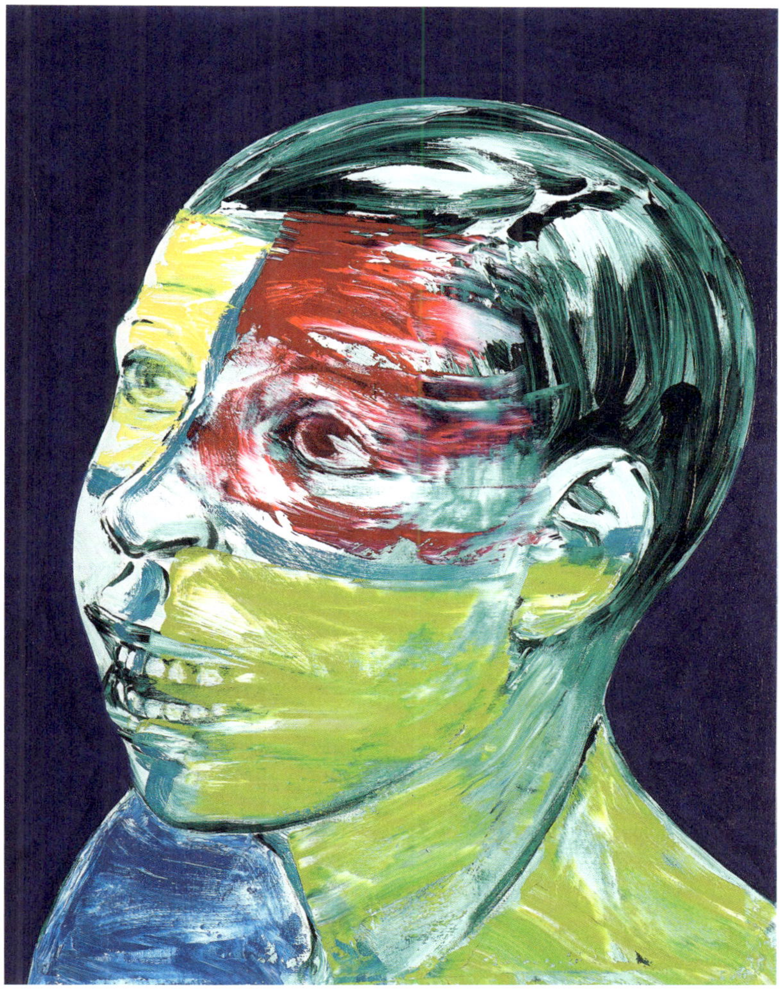

Hypnotiseur / Hypnotist
2020, Öl auf Leinwand, 130 × 100 cm

Mathematiker / Mathematician
2020, Öl auf Leinwand, 130 × 100 cm

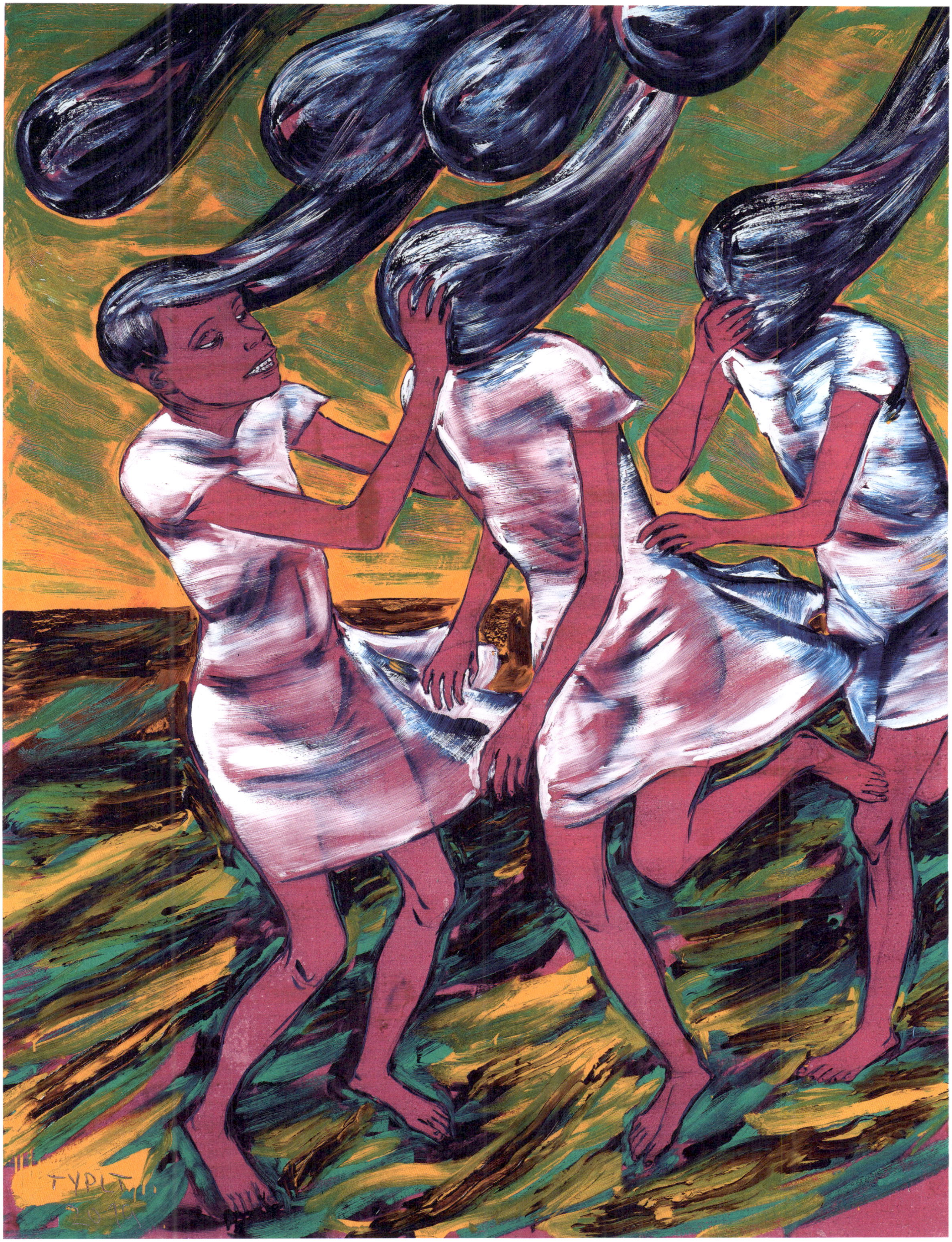

Somnambul / Somnambulistic
2019, Öl auf Leinwand, 240 × 180 cm

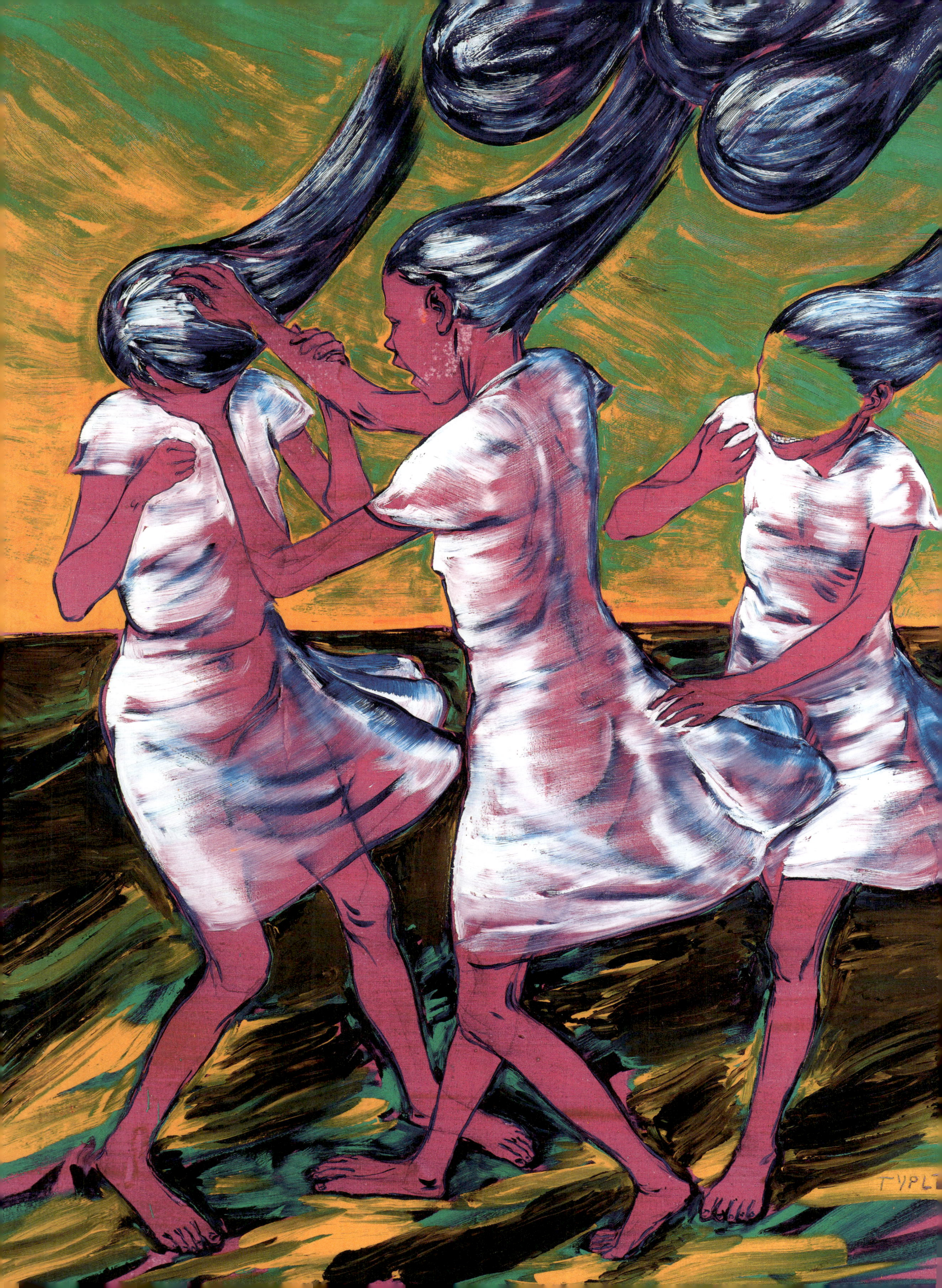

Sekundantinnen / Seconds to the Duel
2019, Öl auf Leinwand, 240 × 180 cm

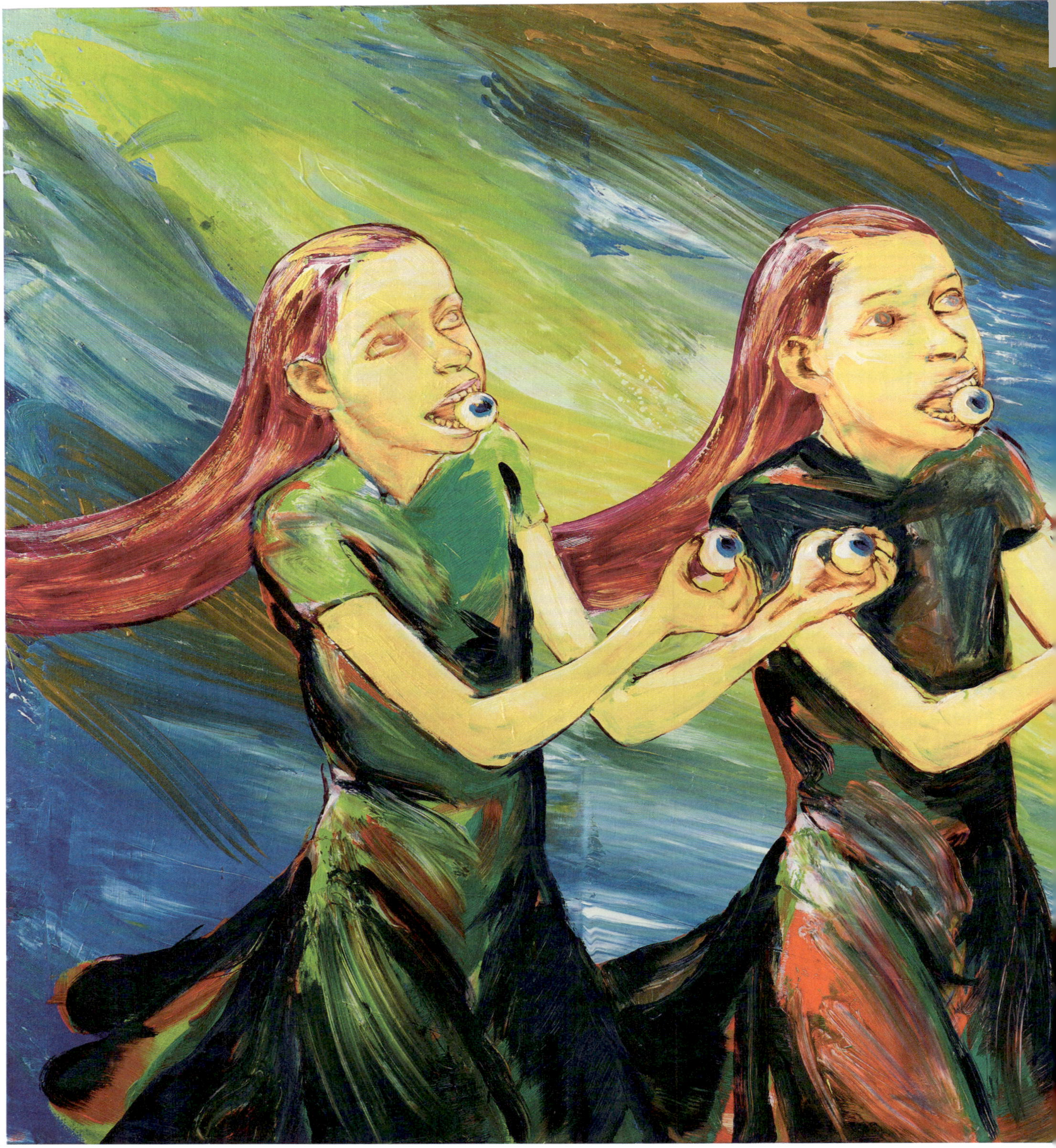

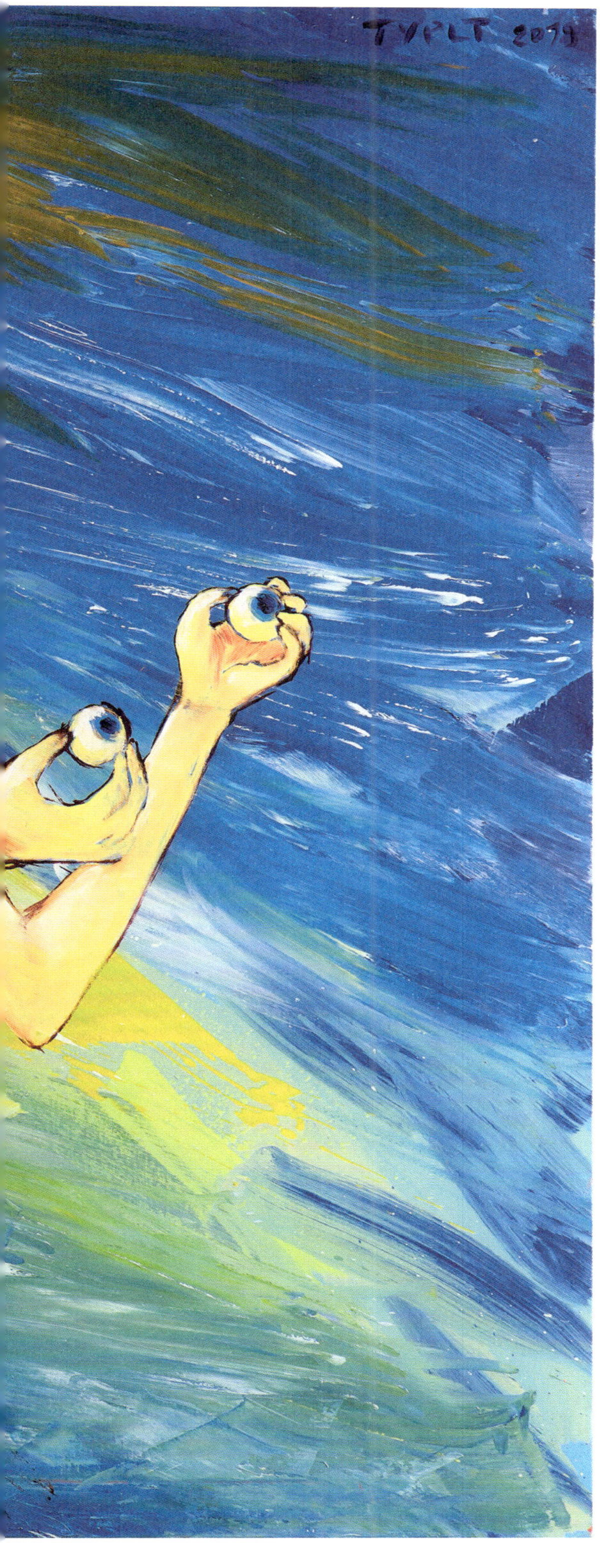

Einzelgängerinnen / Loners
2019, Öl auf Leinwand, 180 × 240 cm

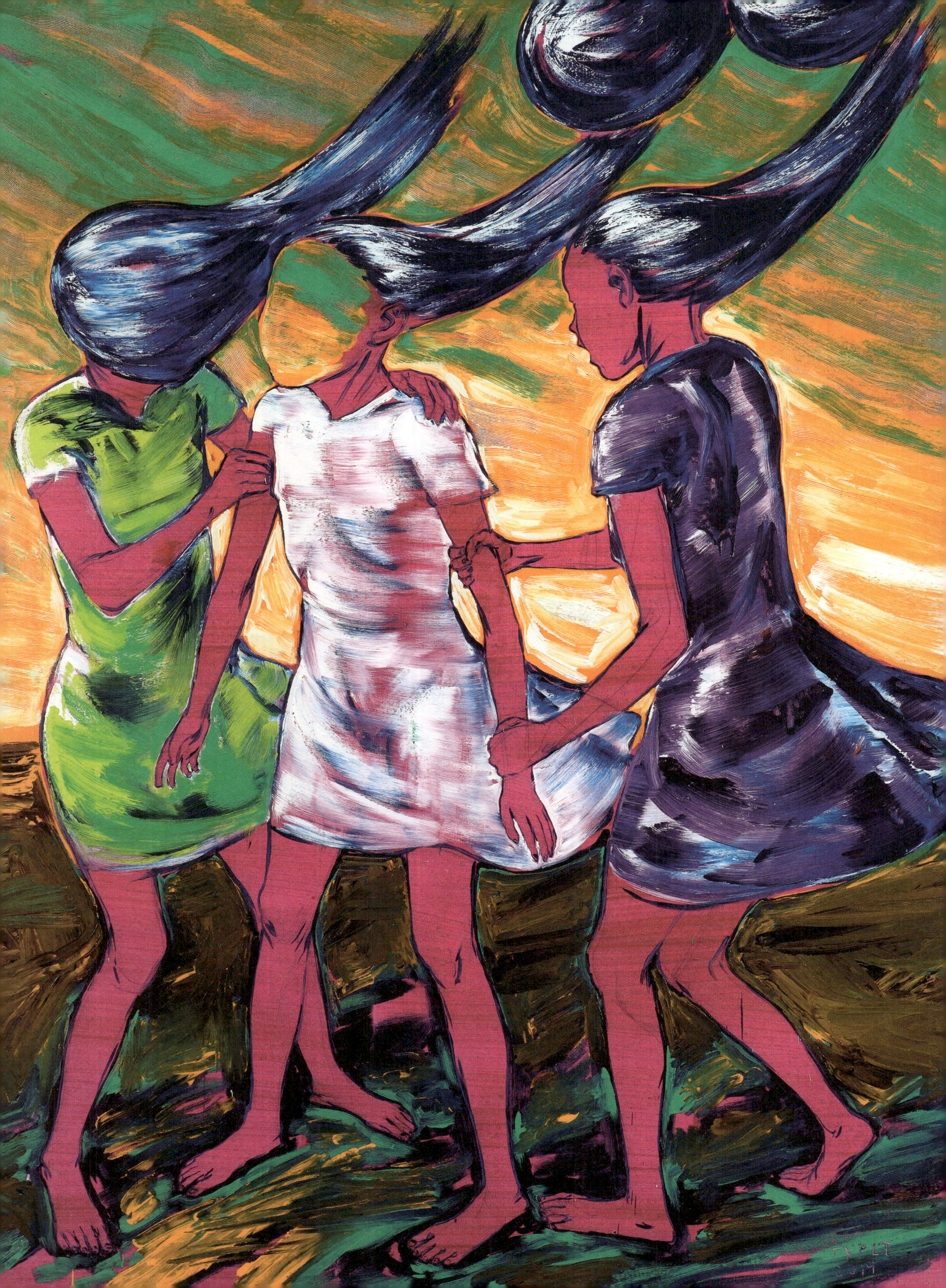

Abendstern / Evening Star
2019, Öl auf Leinwand, 240 × 180 cm

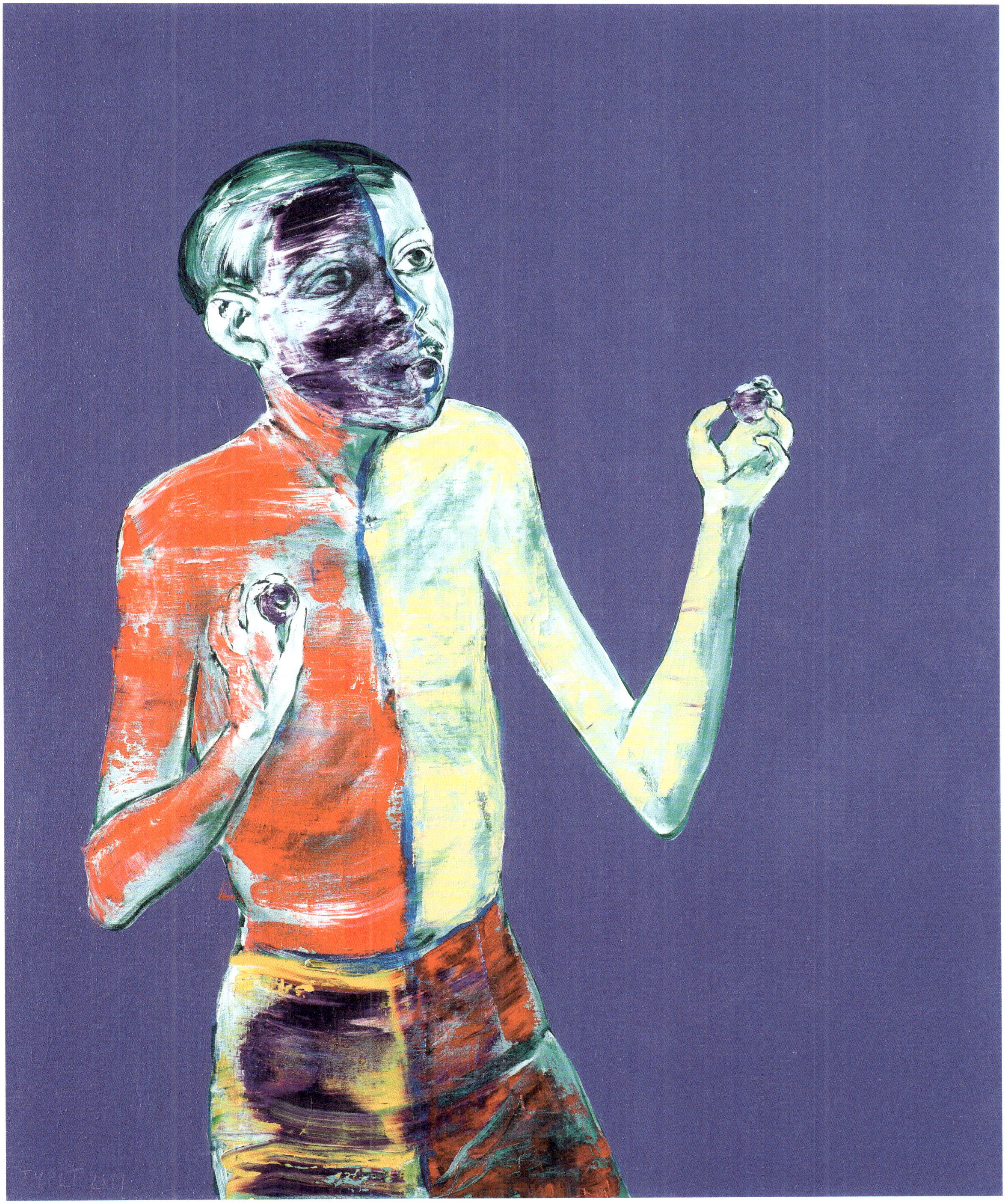

Einzelgänger in Violett / Loner in Purple
2019, Öl auf Leinwand, 160 × 130 cm

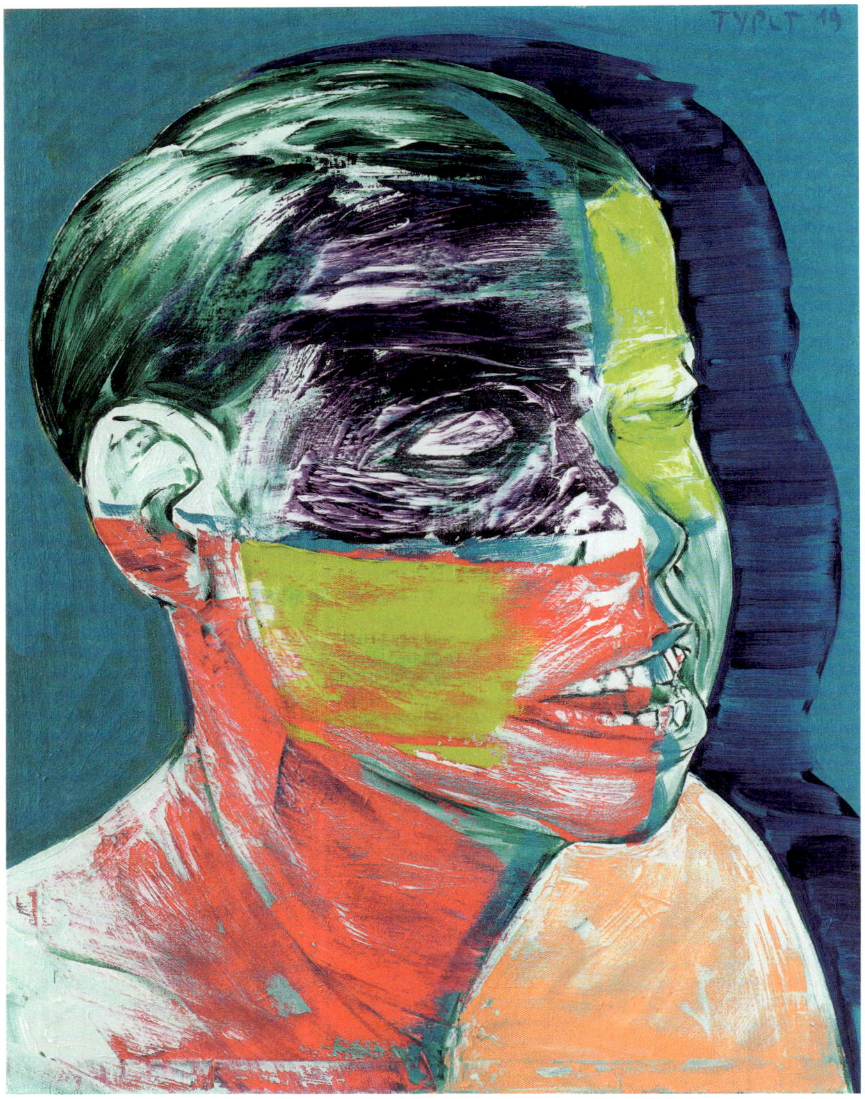

Konterrevolutionär / Counter-Revolutionary
2019, Öl auf Leinwand, 130 × 100 cm

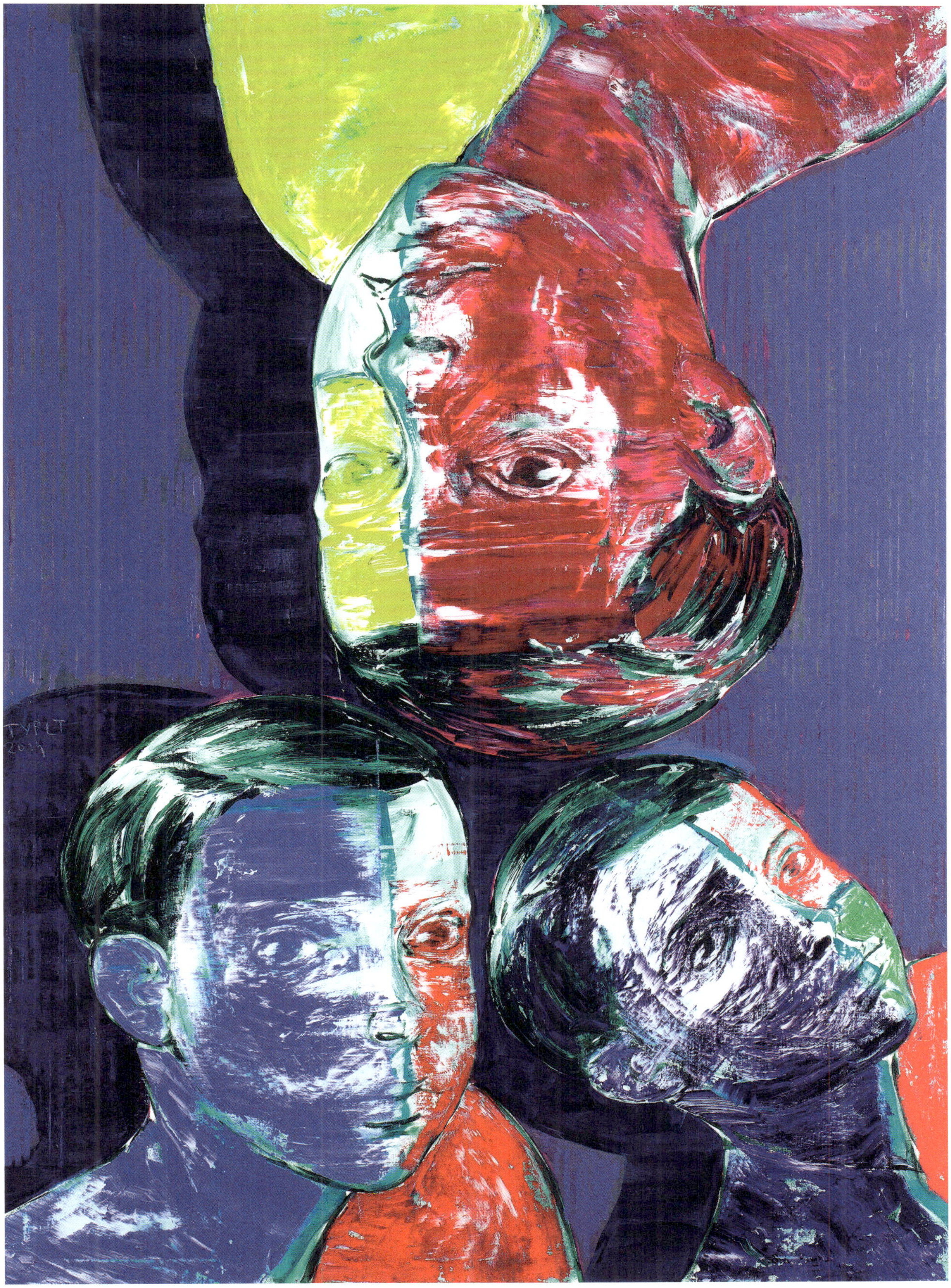

Astronauten / Astronauts
2019, Öl auf Leinwand, 200 × 145 cm

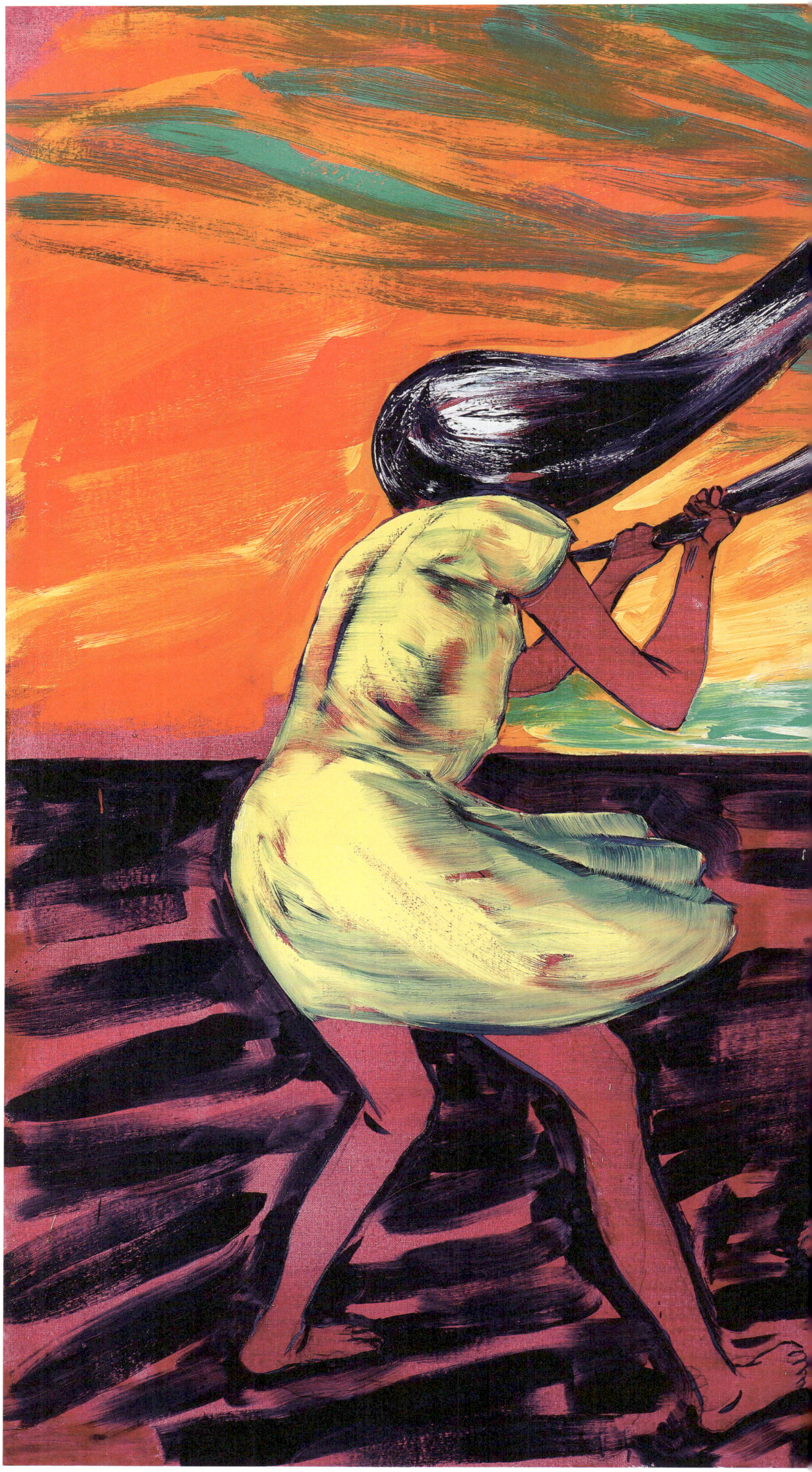

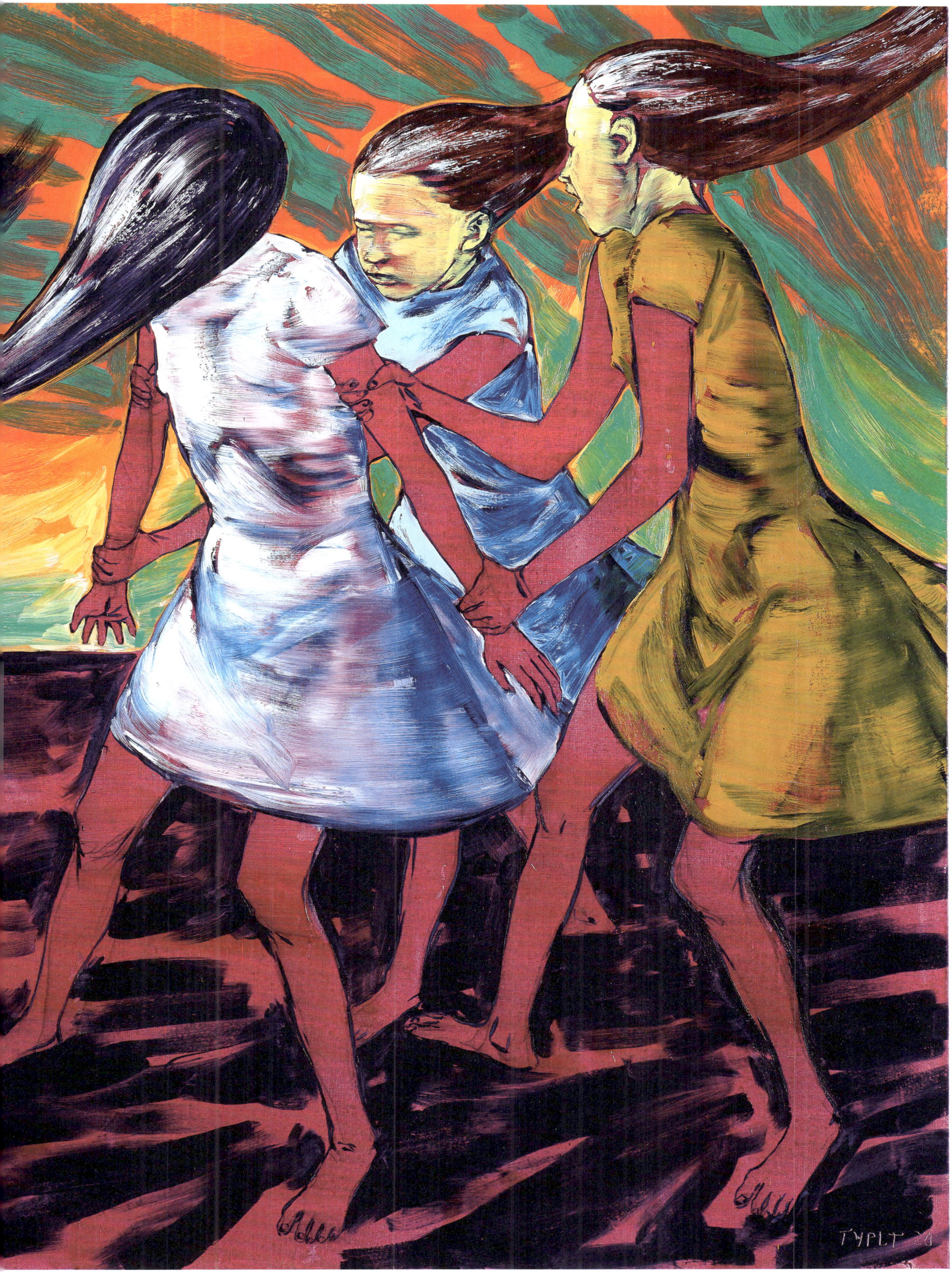

Fusion / Fusion
2020, Öl auf Leinwand, 200 × 260 cm

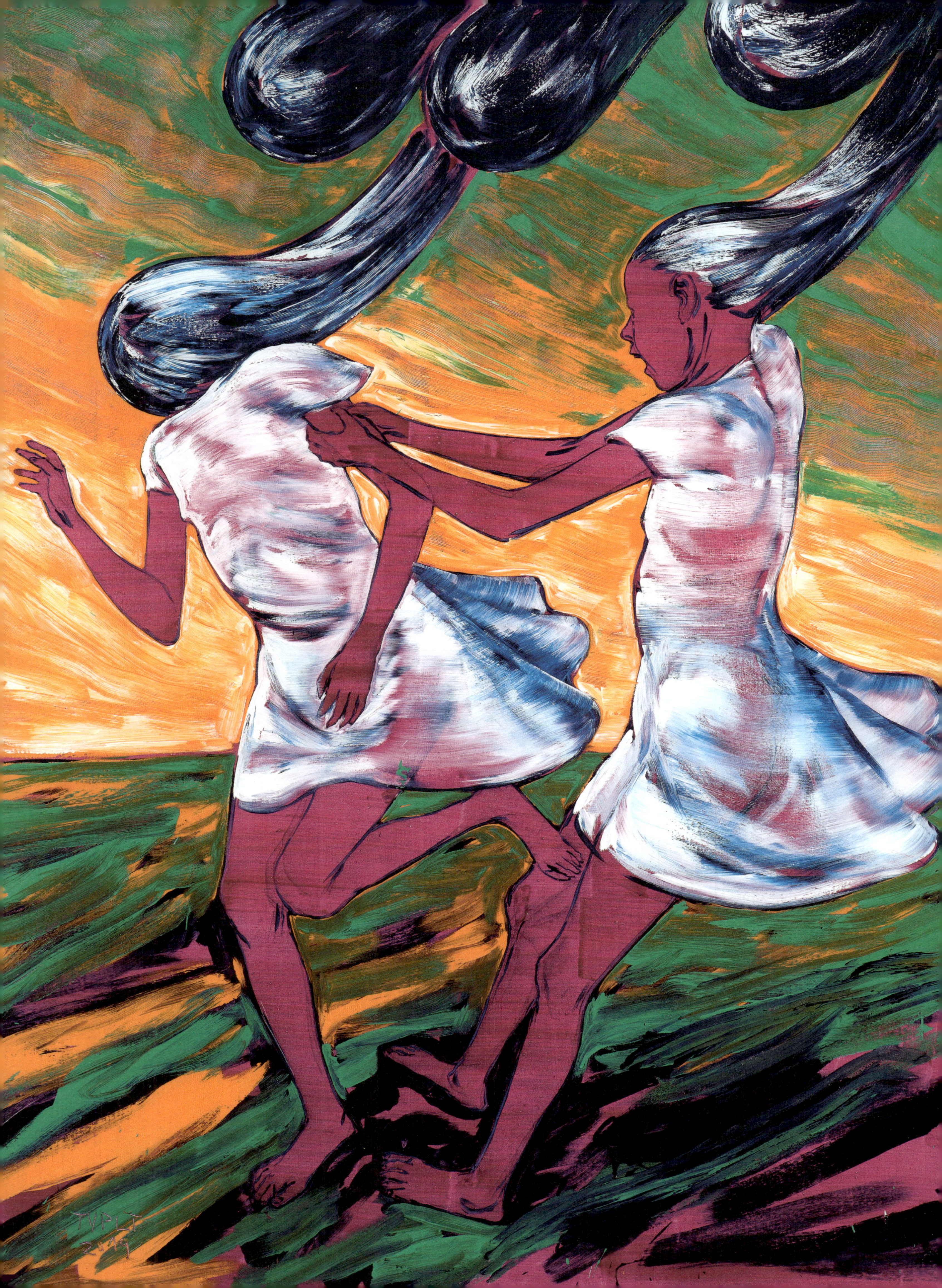

Duell / Duel
2019, Öl auf Leinwand, 240 × 180 cm

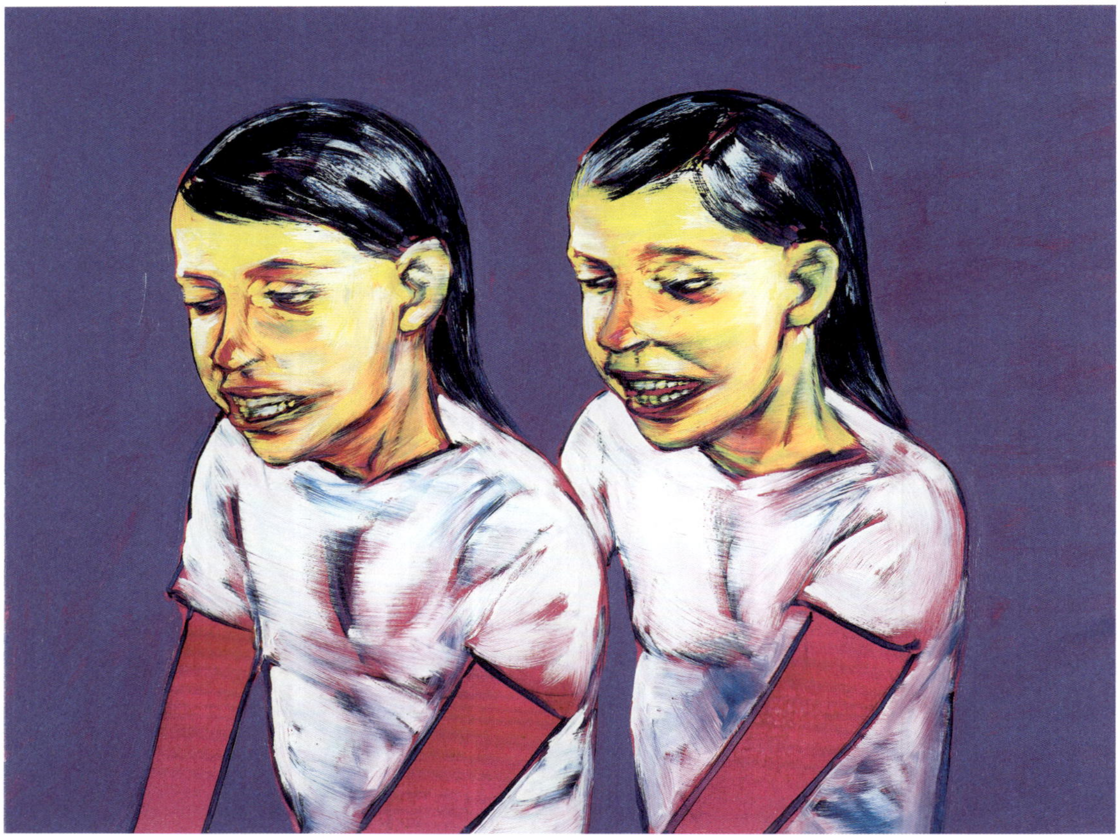

Violetter Dienstag / Purple Tuesday
2020, Öl auf Leinwand, 100 × 130 cm

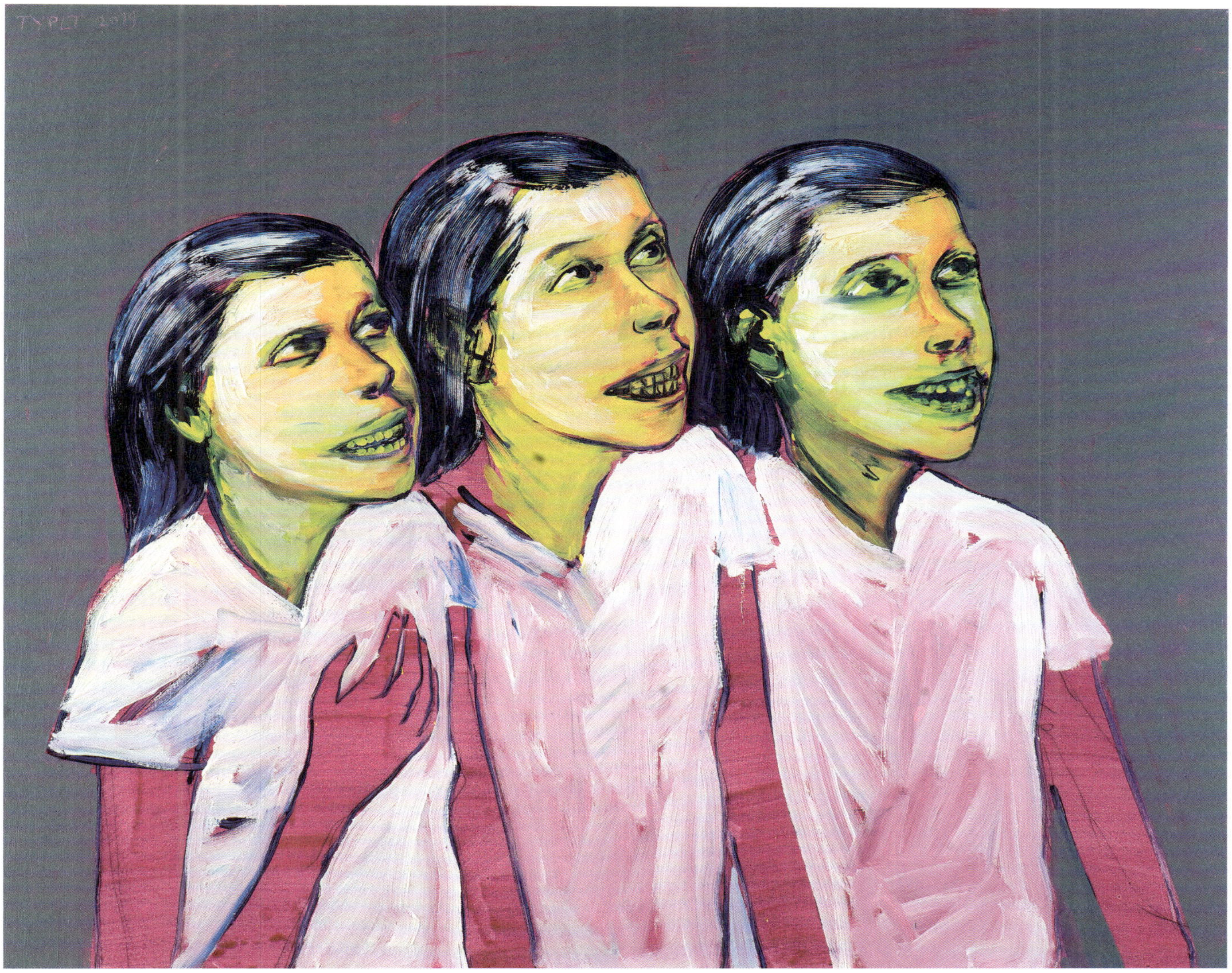

Bleierner Sonntag / Leaden Sunday
2019, Öl auf Leinwand, 130 × 160 cm

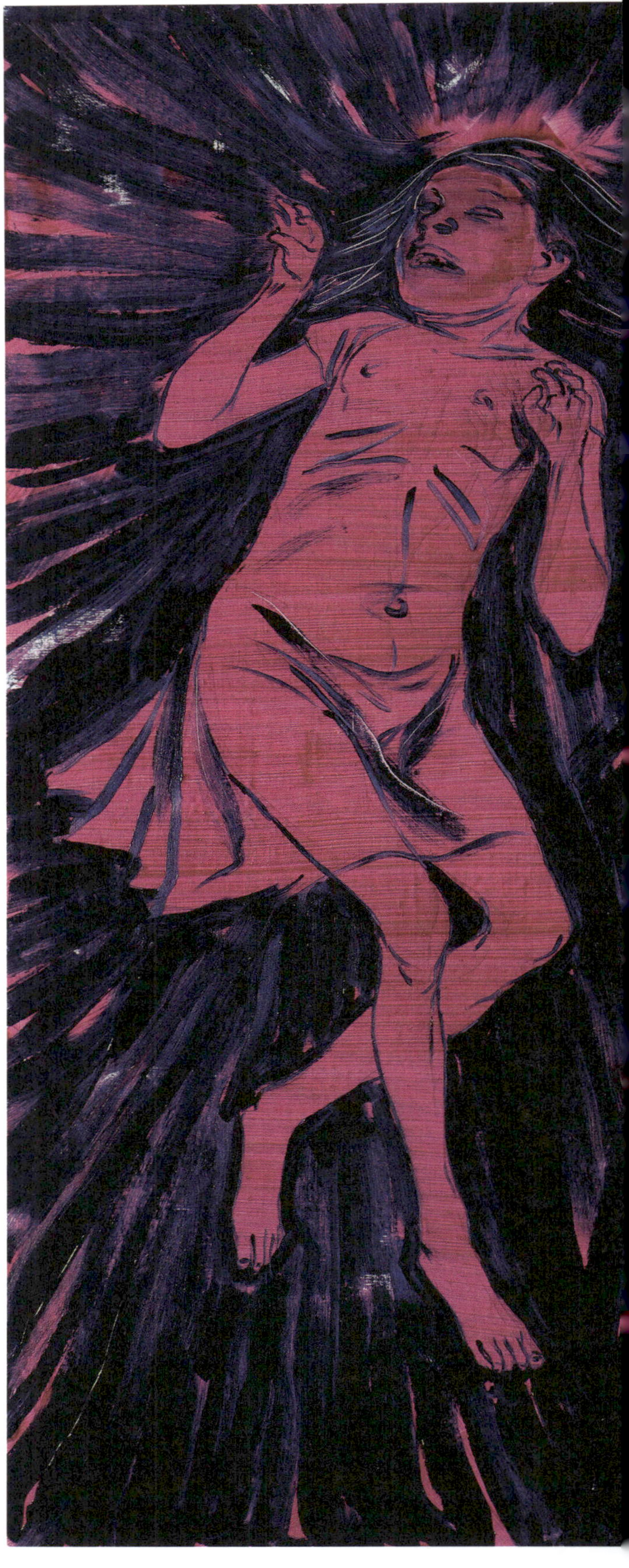

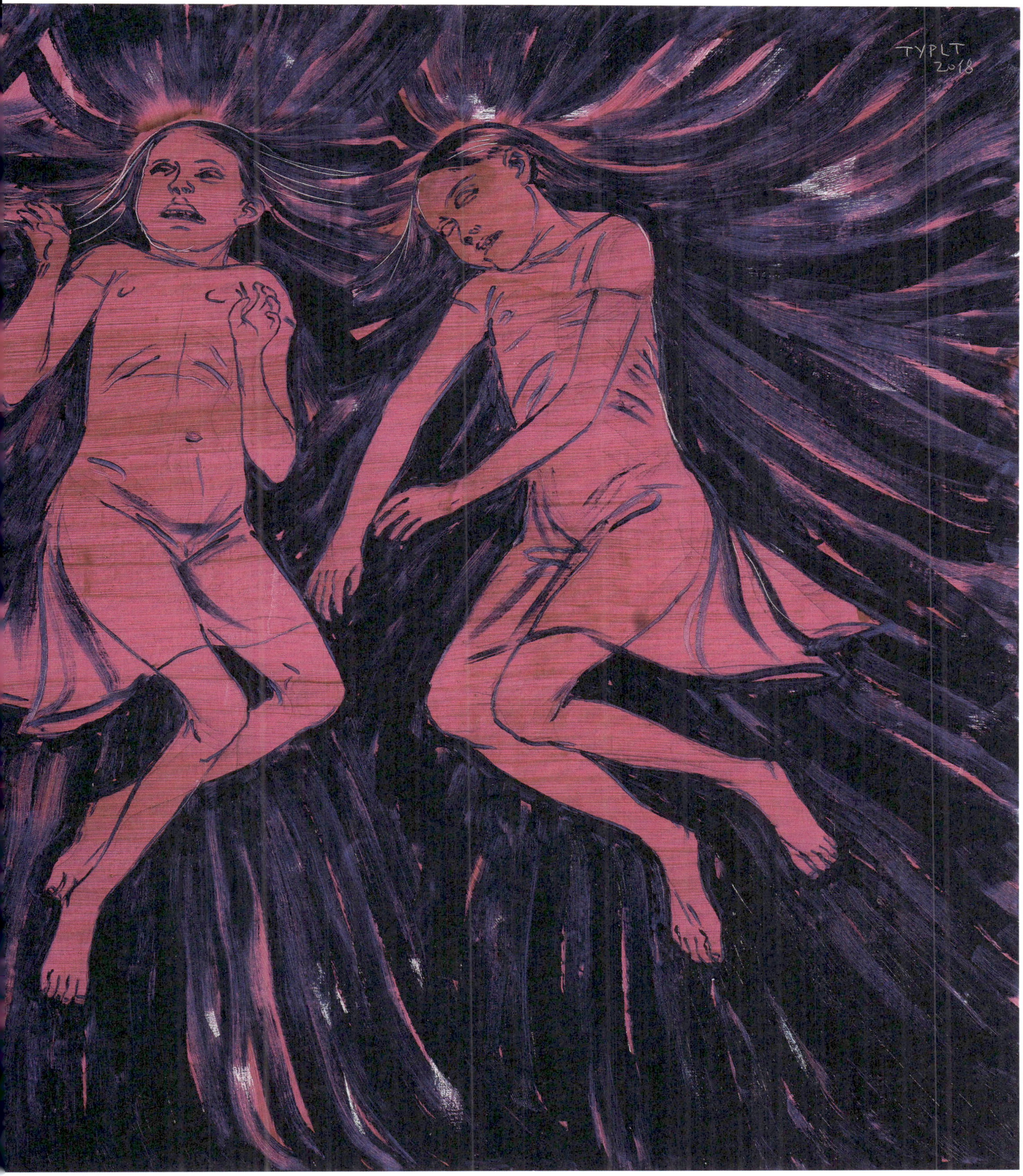

Ich würde der Sonne gern helfen zu brennen / I'd Like to Help the Sun to Shine
2018, Öl auf Leinwand, 200 × 260 cm

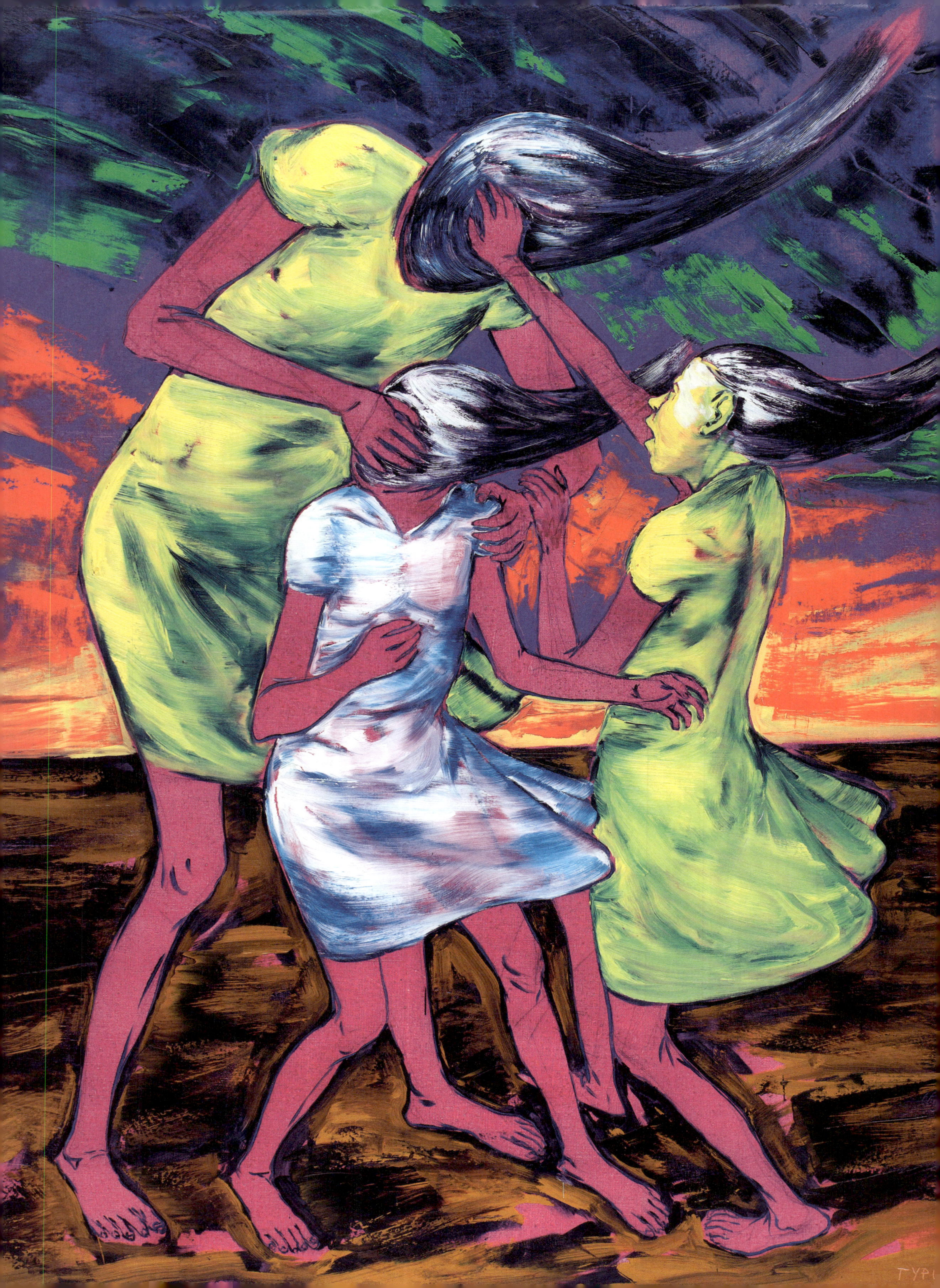

Die Himmelszangen schlossen sich / The Heavens Have Closed their Grip
2020, Öl auf Leinwand, 260 × 200 cm

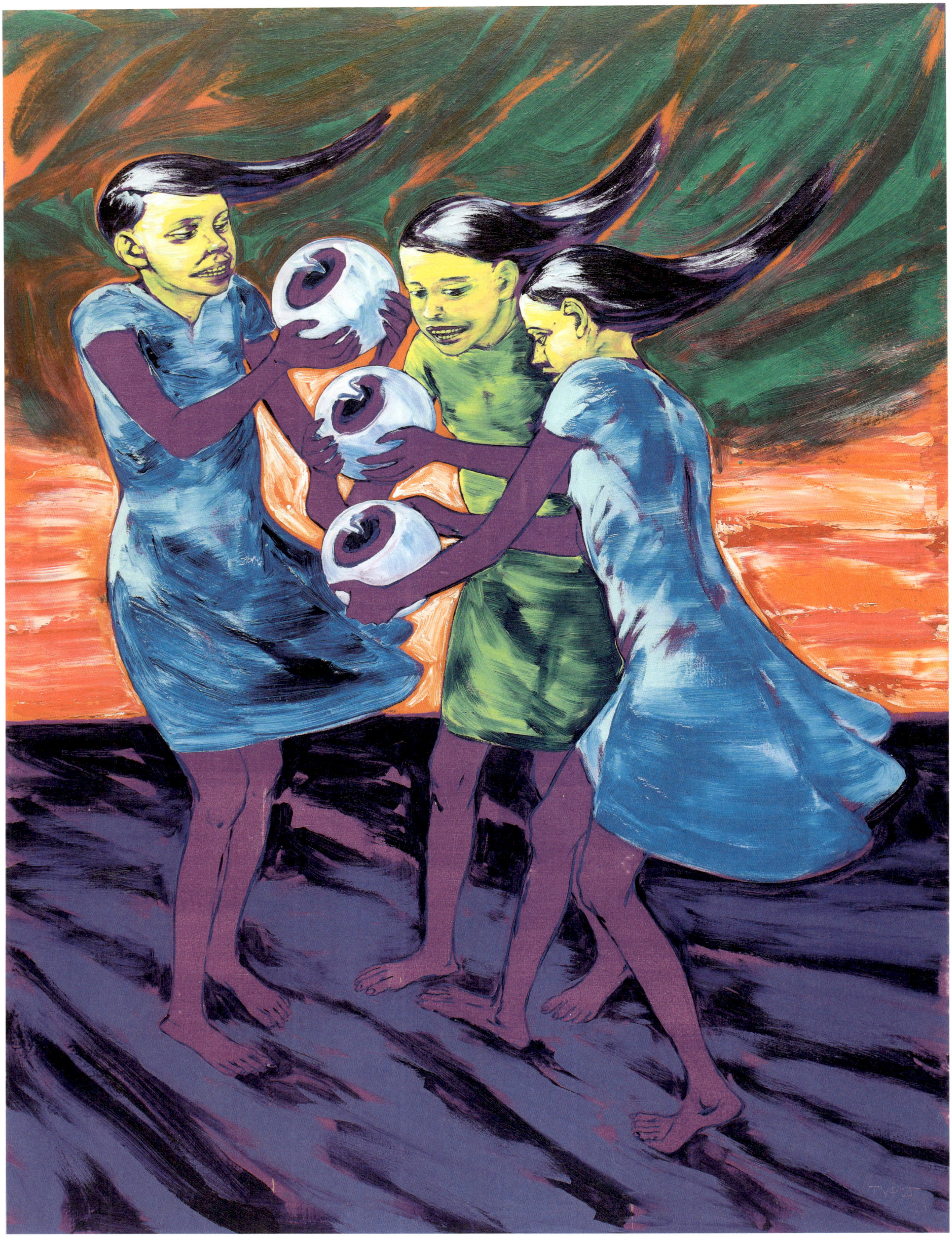

Um einen Schritt näher / One Step Closer
2020, Öl auf Leinwand, 240 × 180 cm

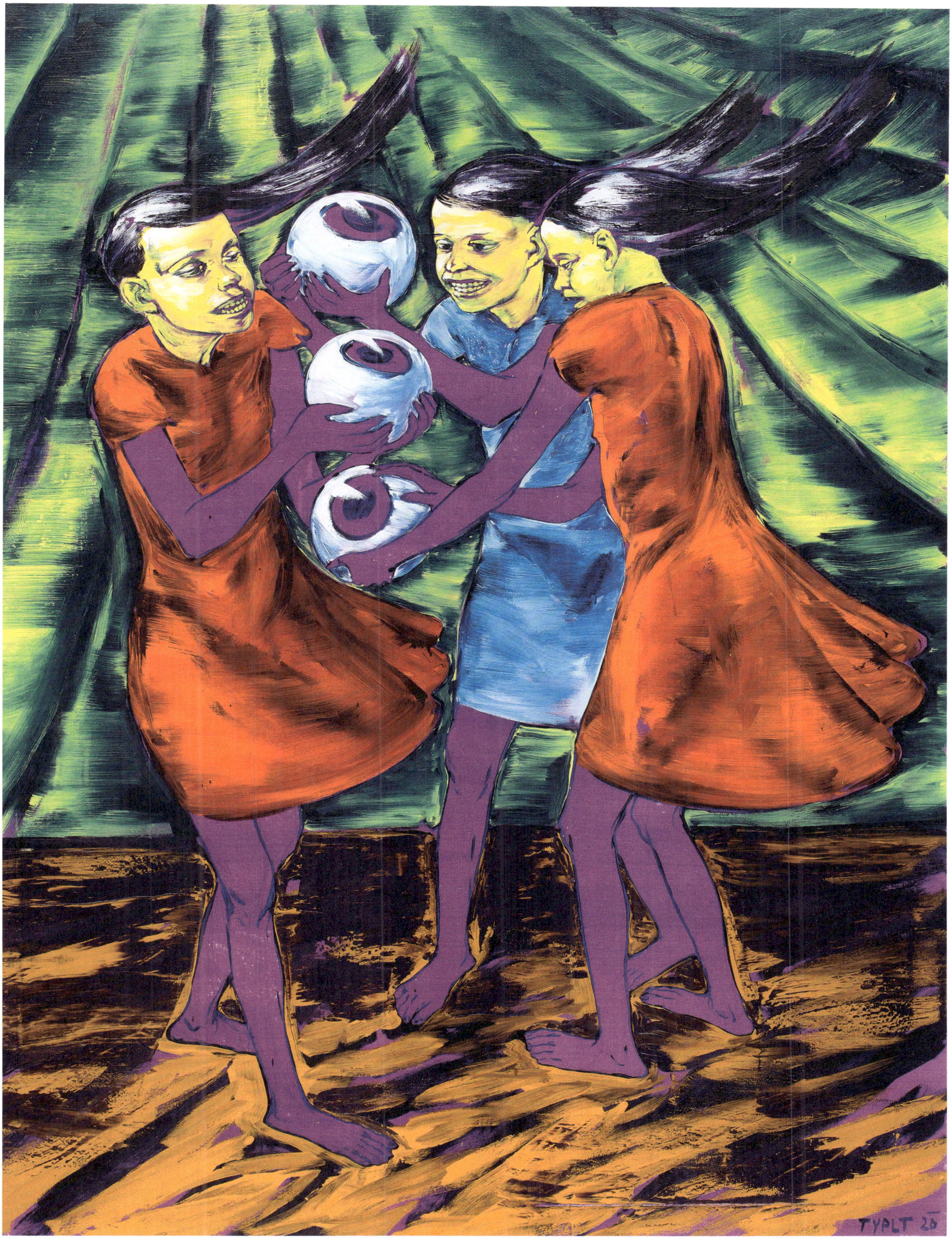

Spaltung / Split
2020, Öl auf Leinwand, 240 × 180 cm

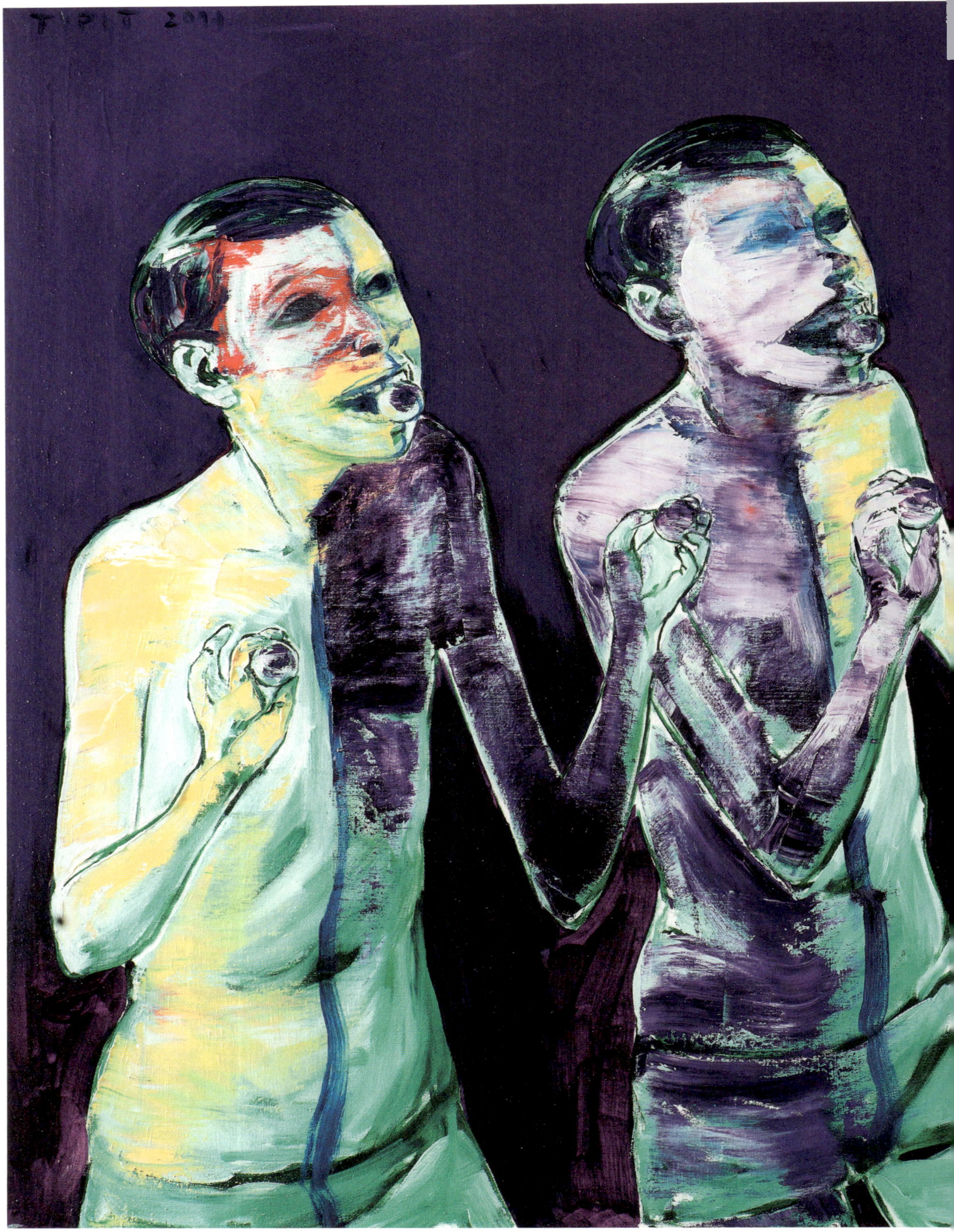

Zu Hause / At Home
2020, Öl auf Leinwand, 145 × 200 cm

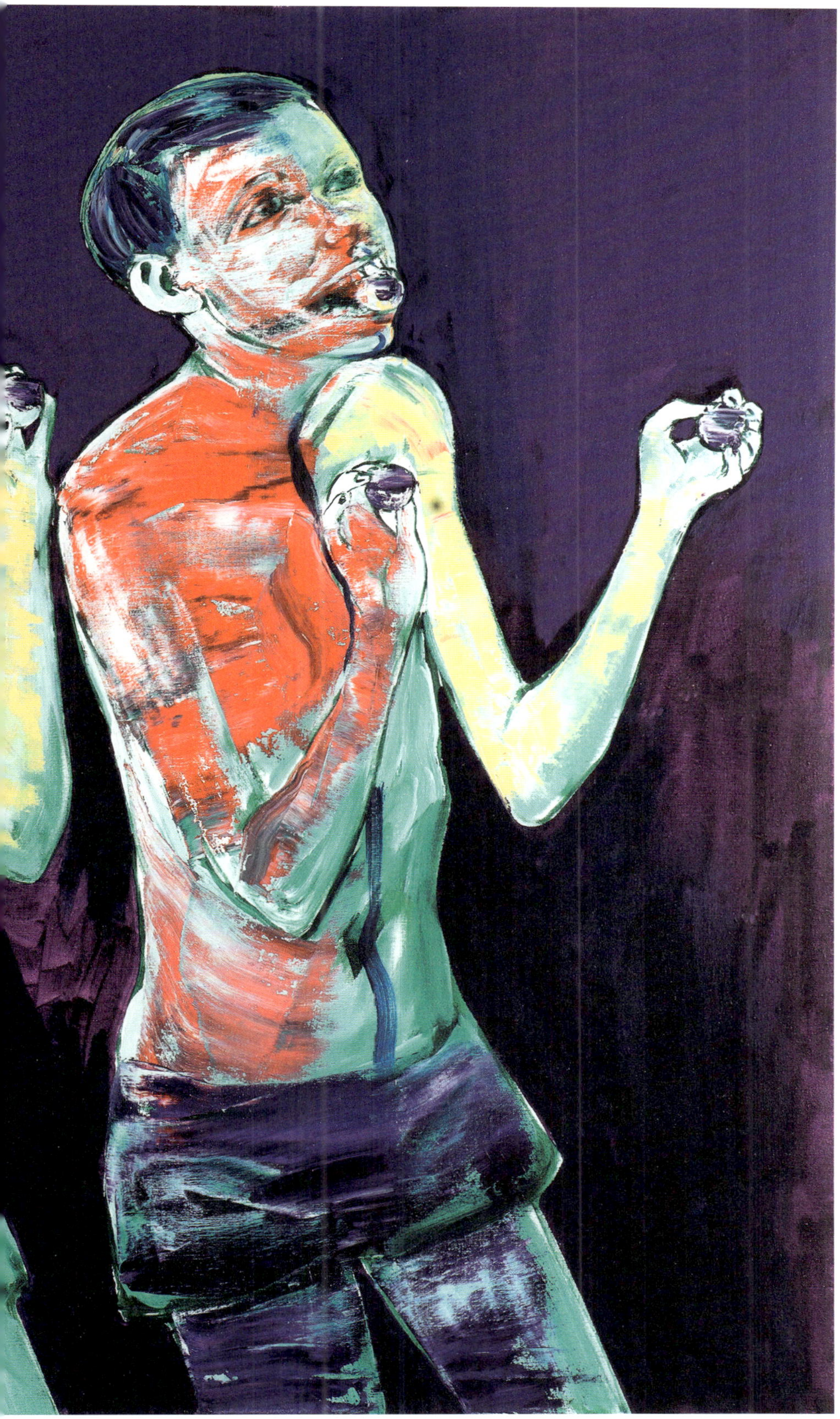

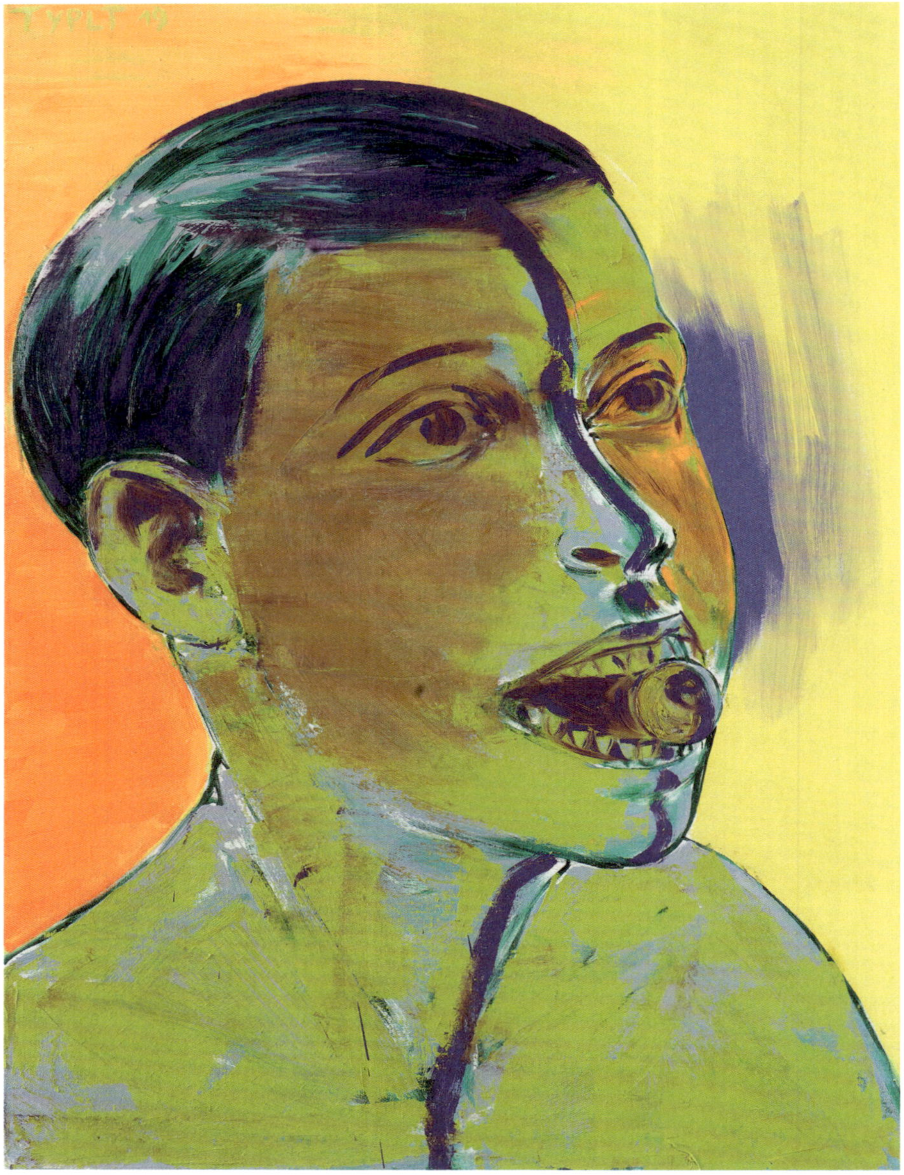

Violette Grenze / Purple Border
2019, Öl auf Leinwand, 140 × 105 cm

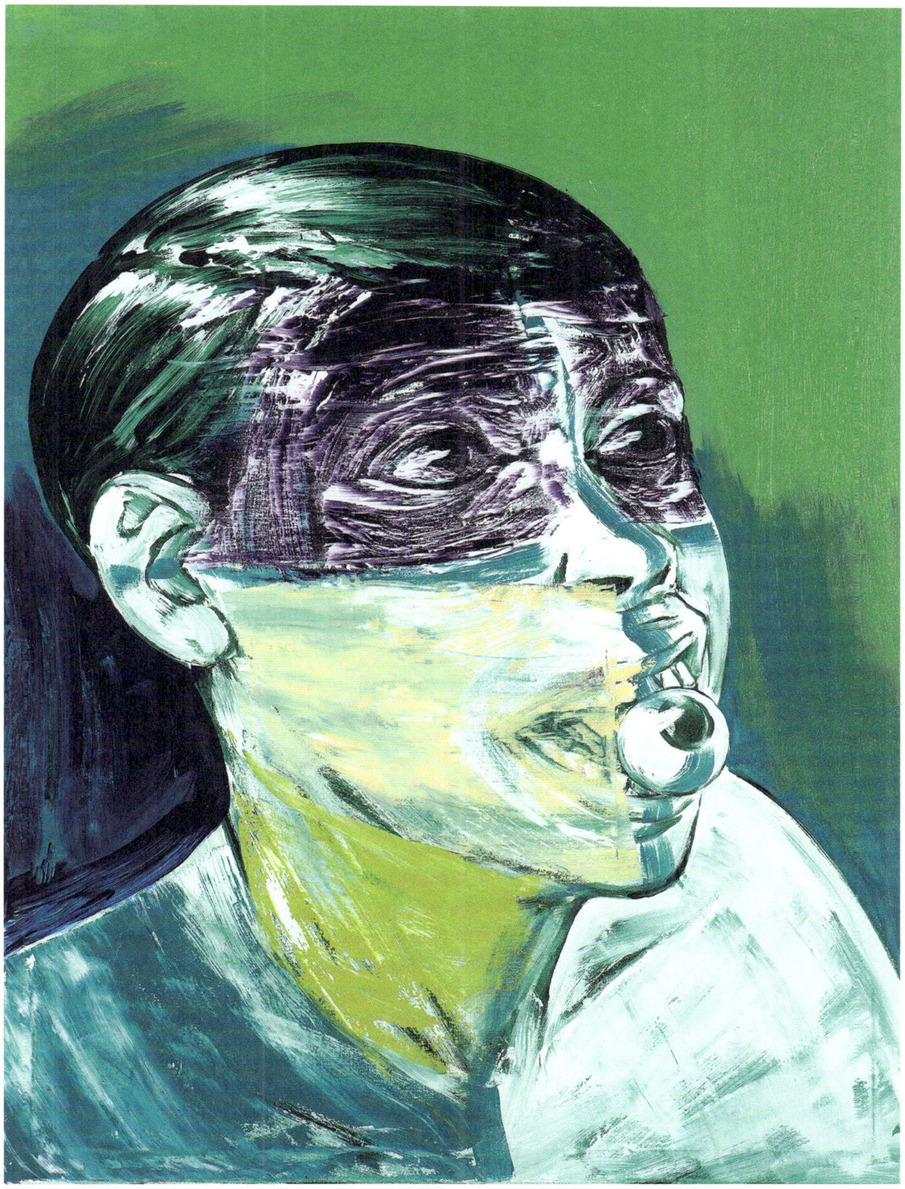

Violetter Hypnotiseur / Purple Hypnotist
2020, Öl auf Leinwand, 140 × 105 cm

Die Zeit beugte sich im Bunde / Time Has Leant Forward
2020, Öl auf Leinwand, 240 × 180 cm

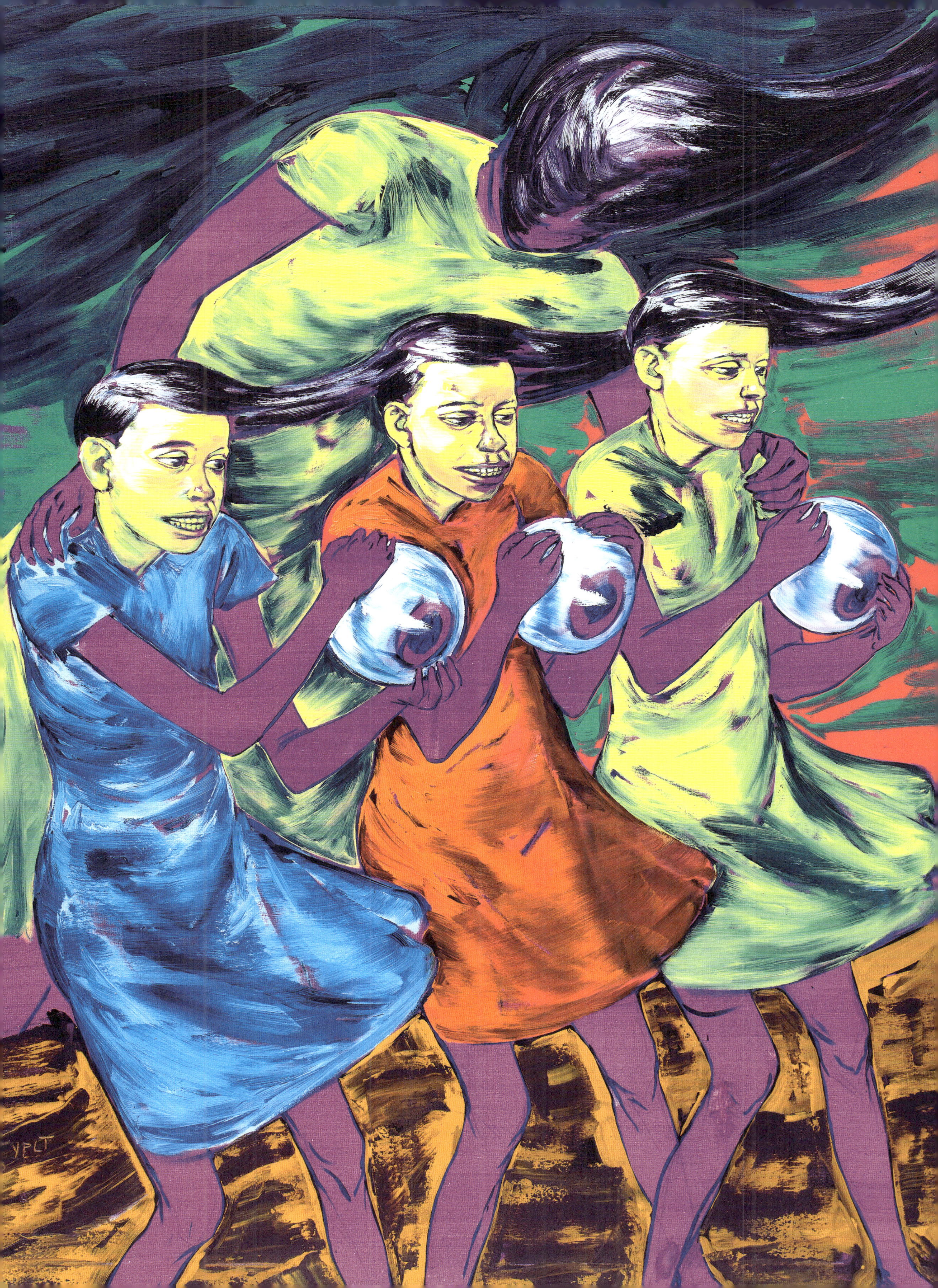
YPLT

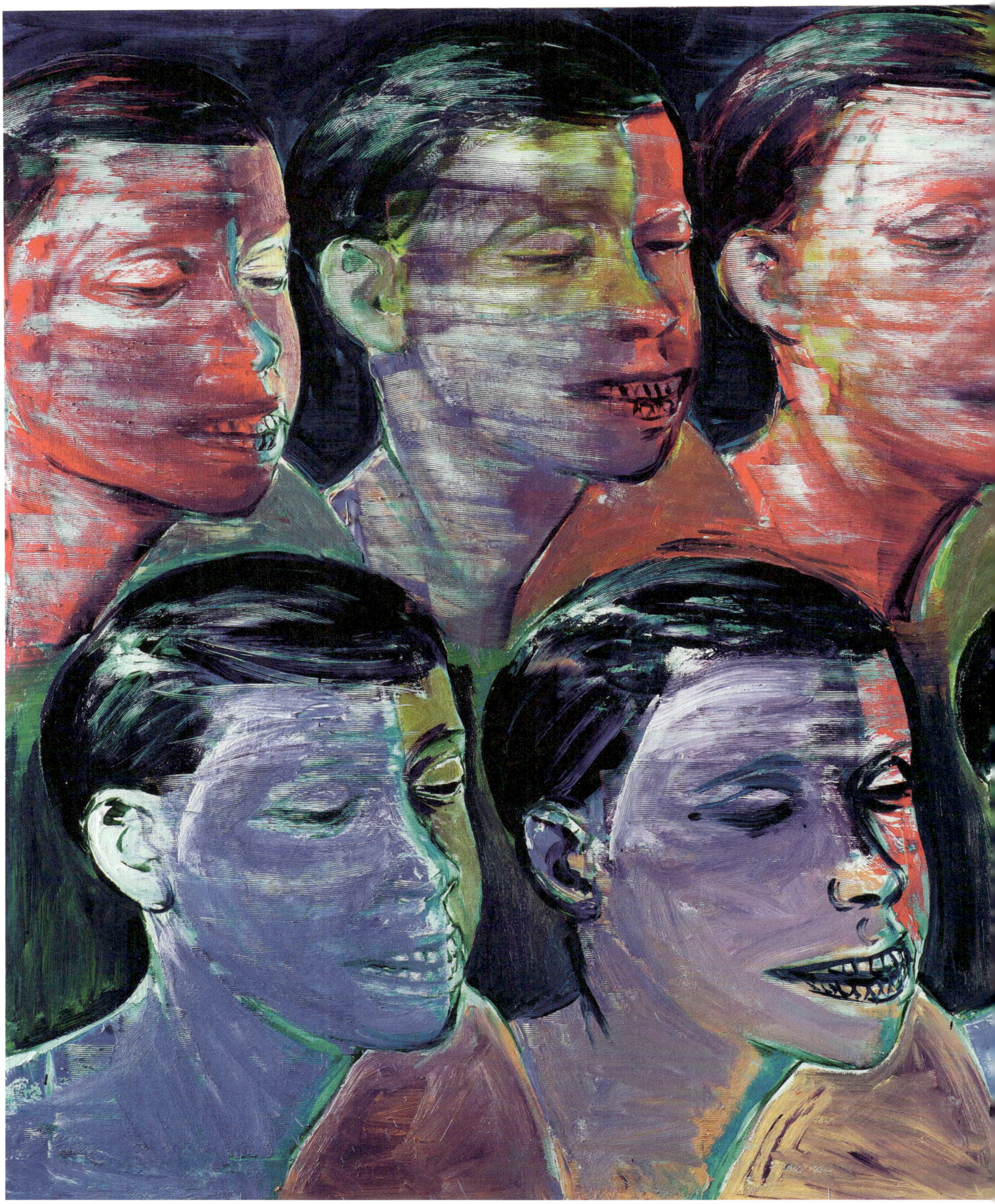

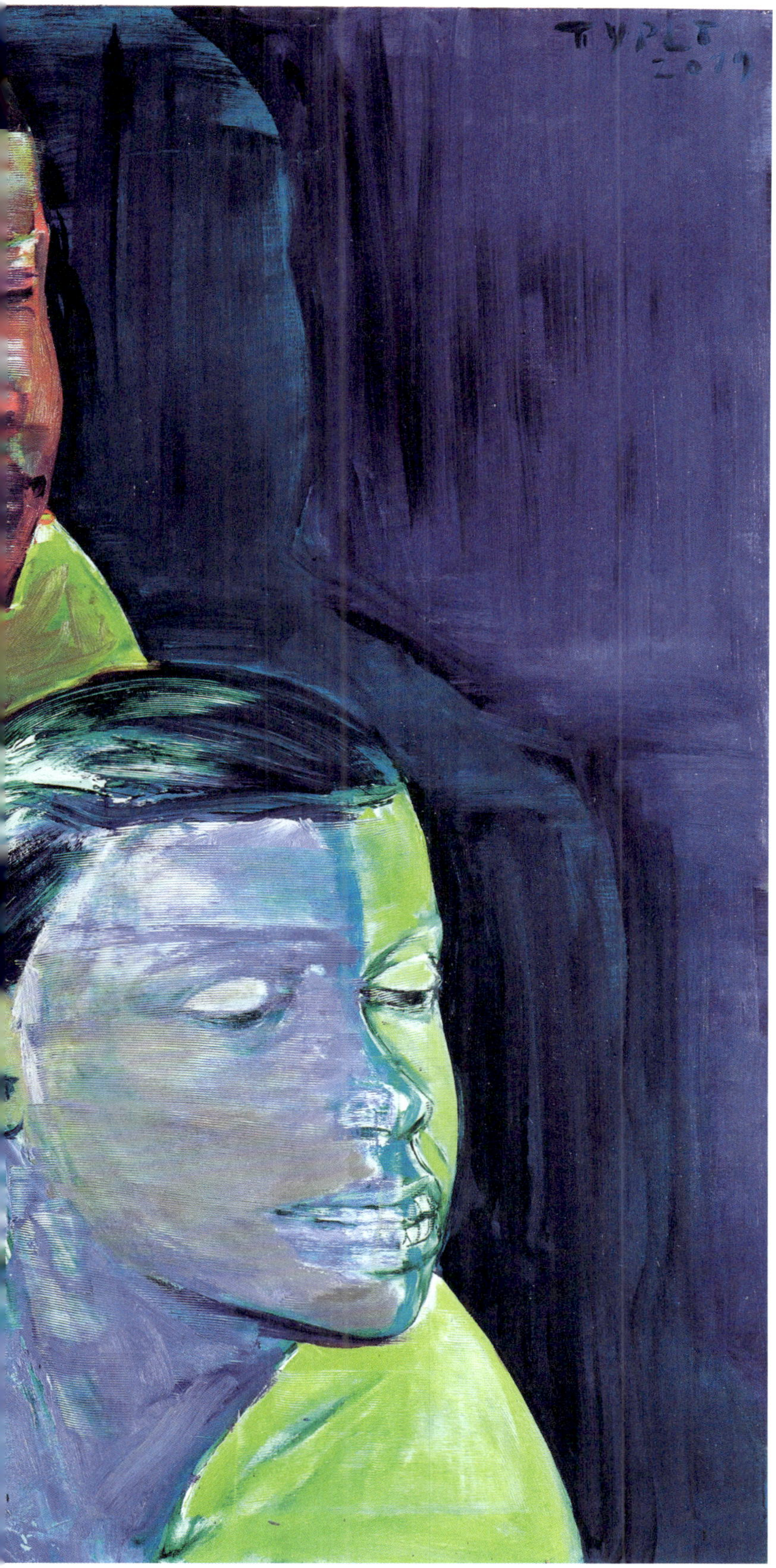

Patrioten / Patriots
2019, Öl auf Leinwand, 180 × 240 cm

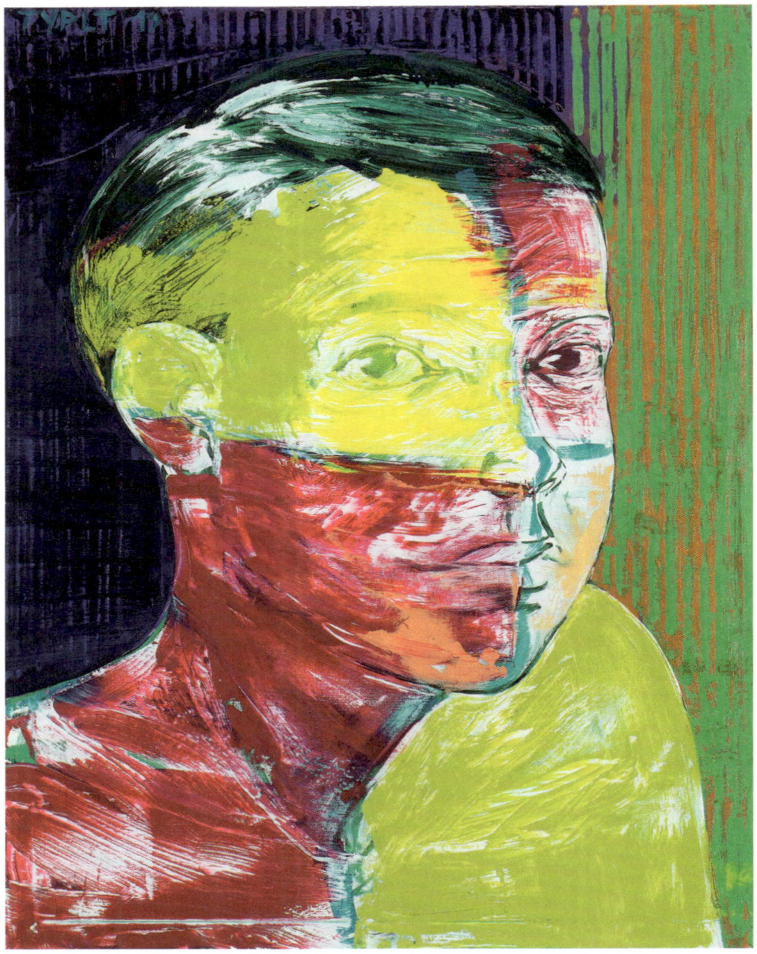

Pataphysiker / Pataphysicist
2019, Öl auf Leinwand, 130 × 100 cm

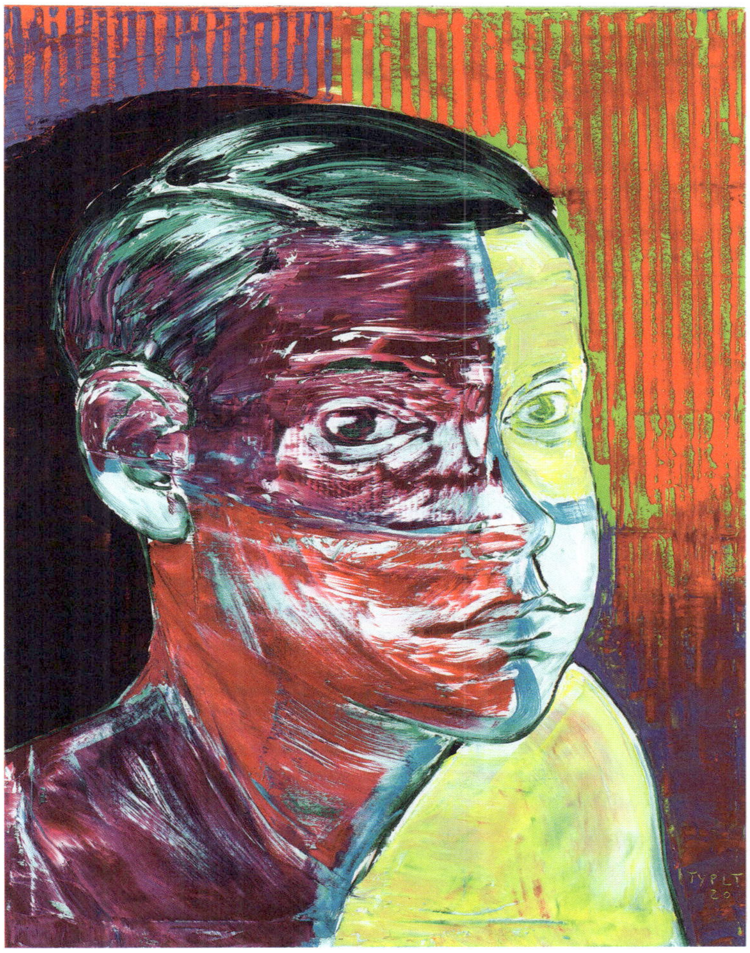

Erster Sekundant / Primary Second to the Duel
2020, Öl auf Leinwand, 130 × 100 cm

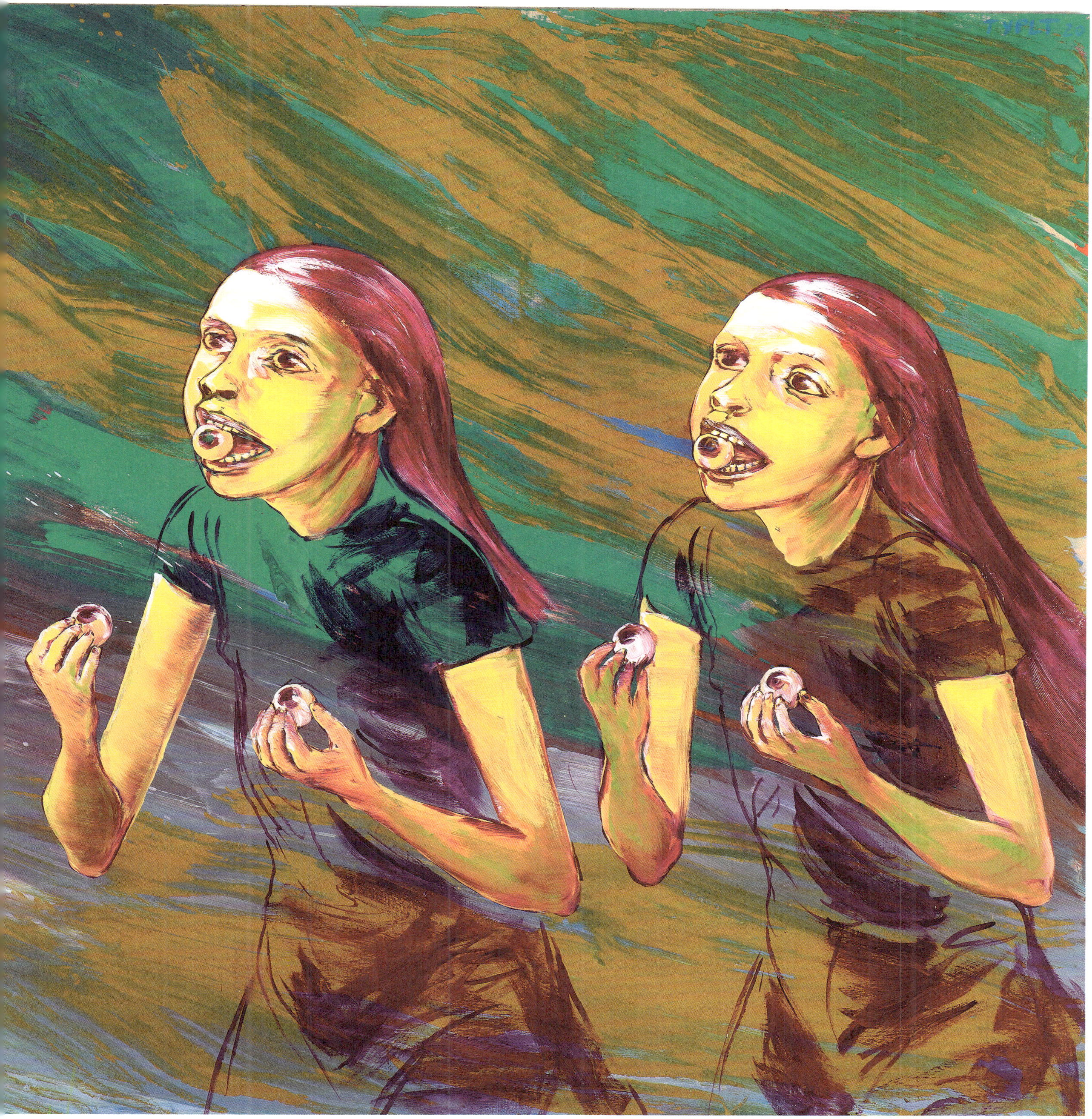

Mein Gesicht hat tausend Augen / My Face Has a Thousand Eyes
2020, Öl auf Leinwand, 180 × 240 cm

Beton / Concrete
2020, Öl auf Leinwand, 240 × 180 cm

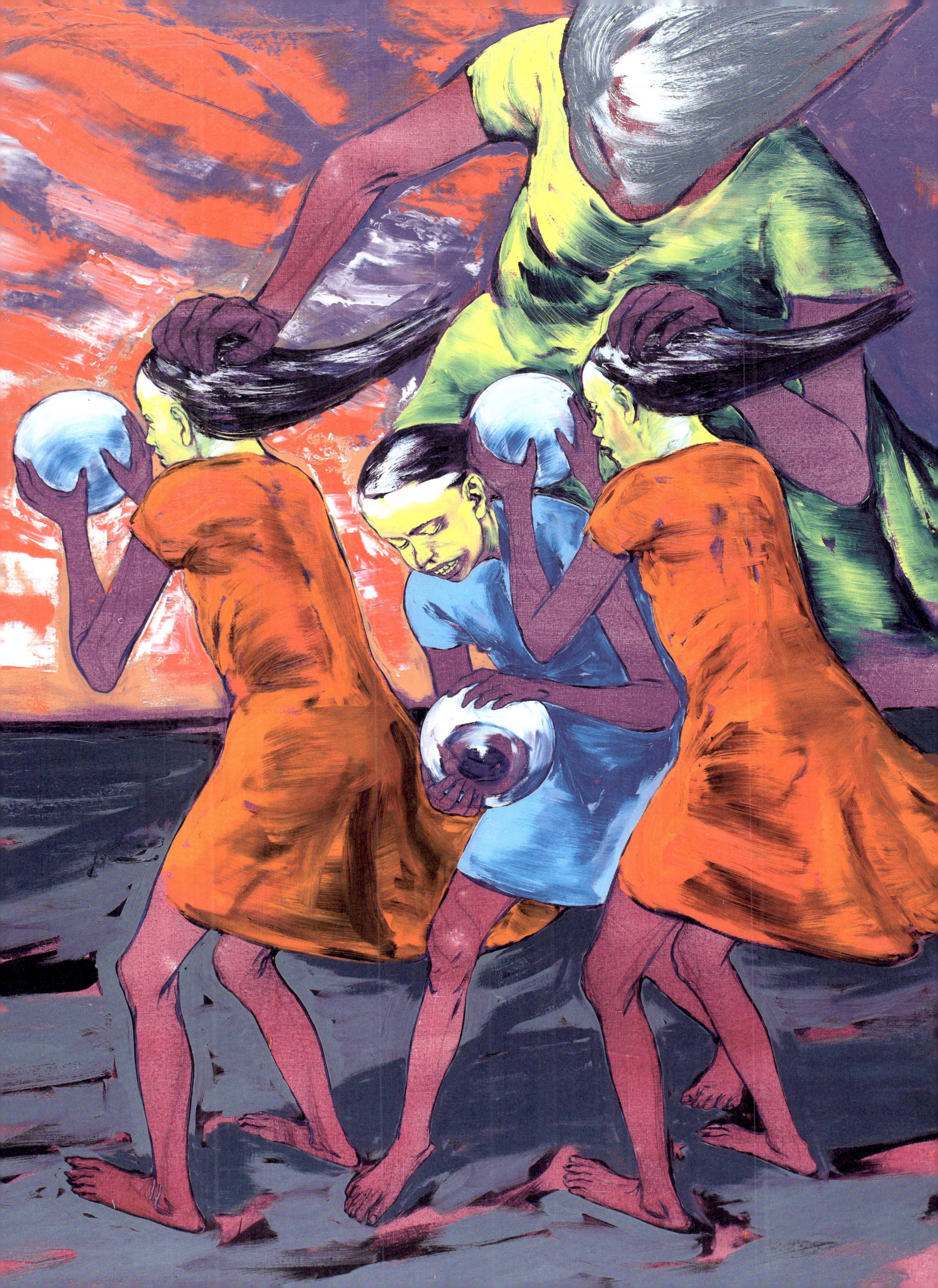

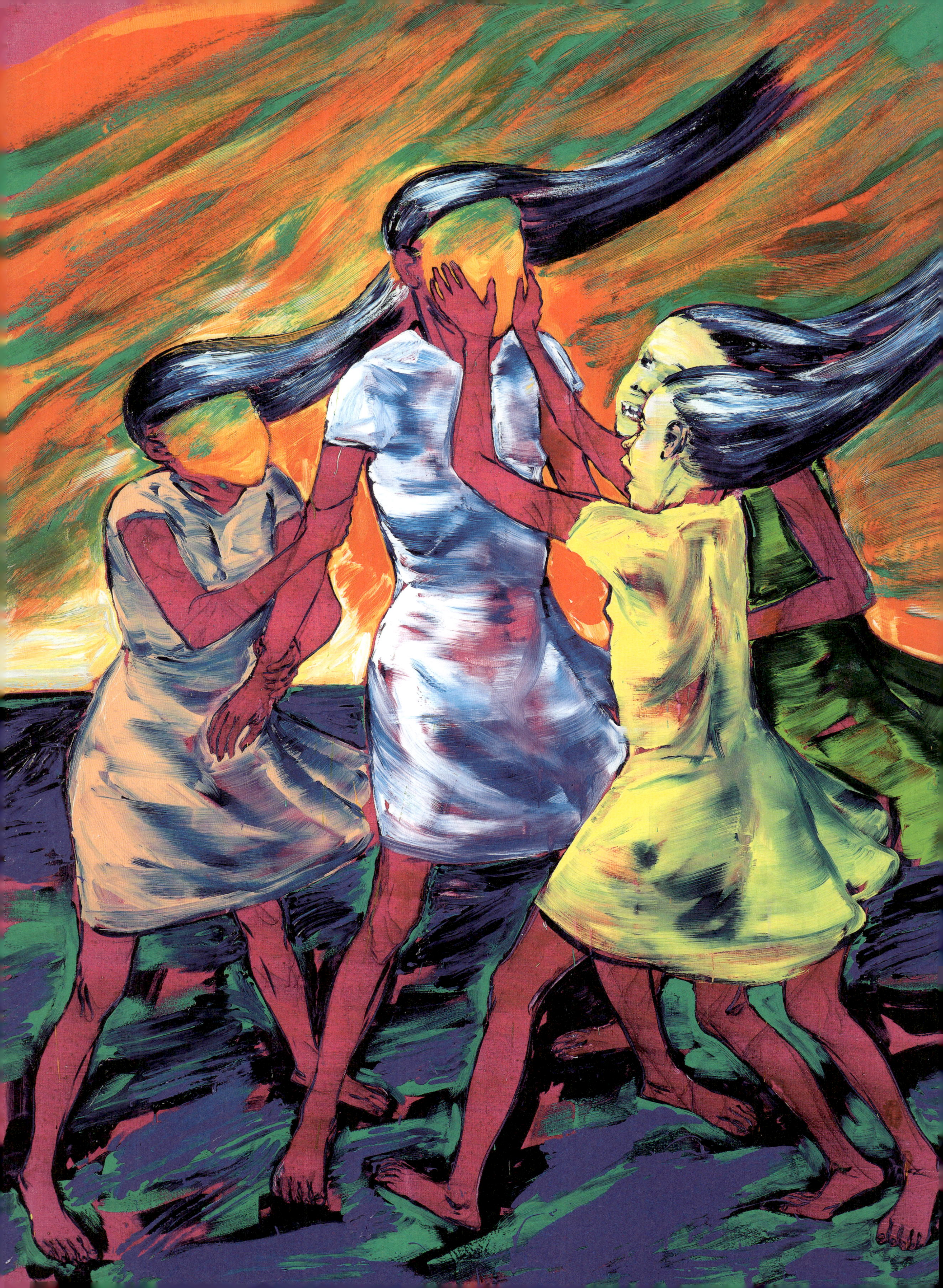

Vertikale Fusion / Vertical Fusion
2020, Öl auf Leinwand, 260 × 200 cm

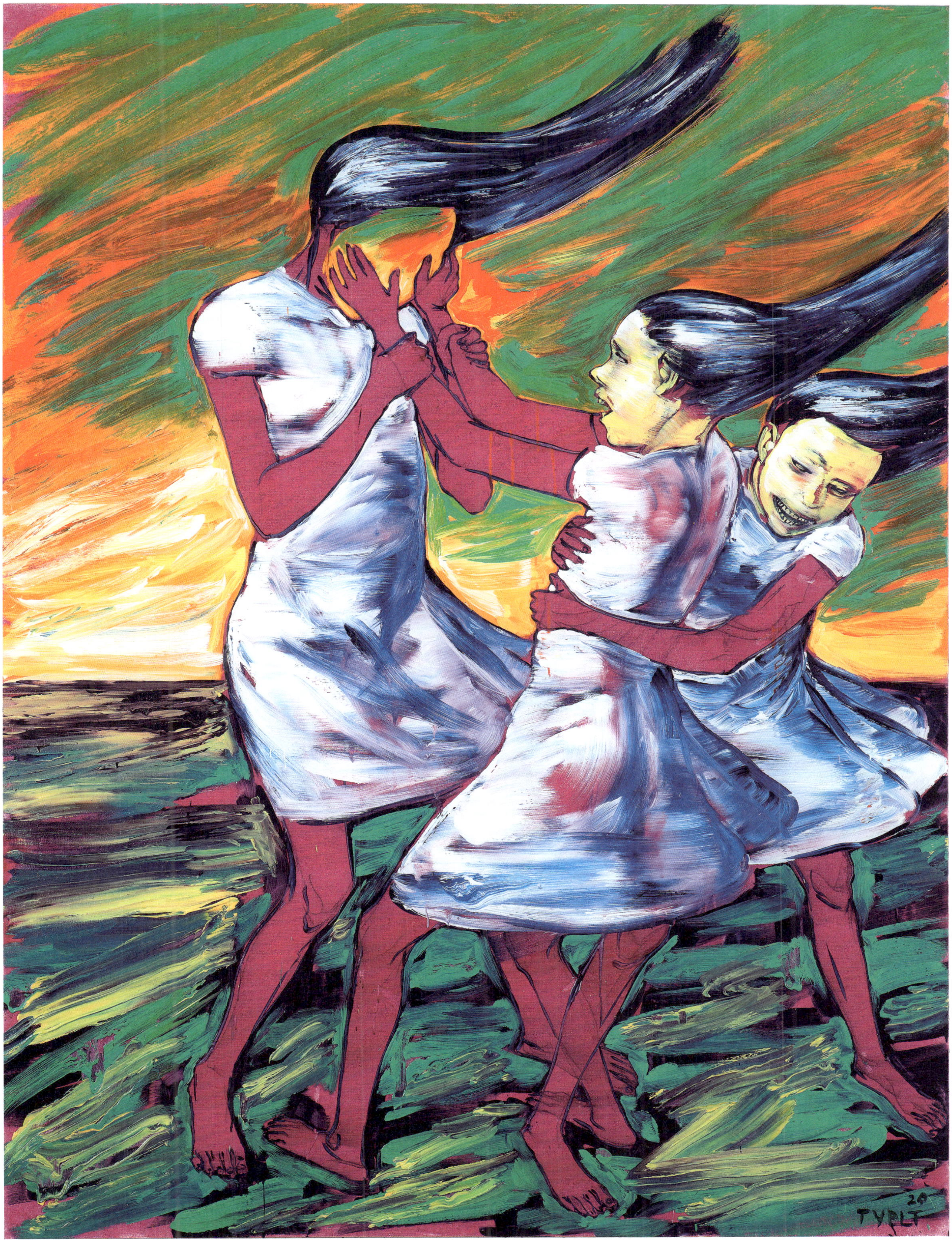

Große Fusion / Great Fusion
2020, Öl auf Leinwand, 240 × 180 cm

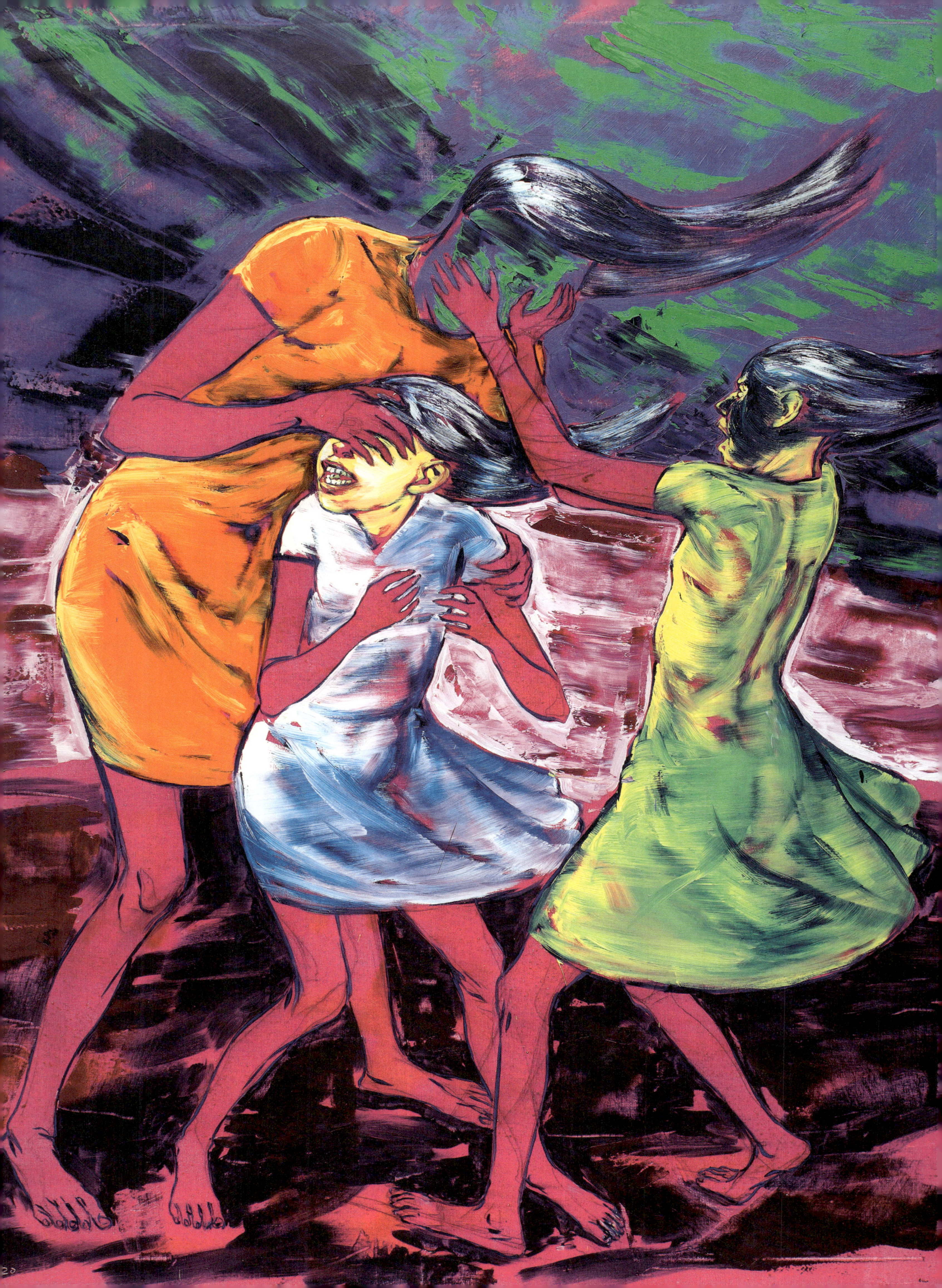

Nächtliche Fusion / Nocturnal Fusion
2020, Öl auf Leinwand, 260 × 200 cm

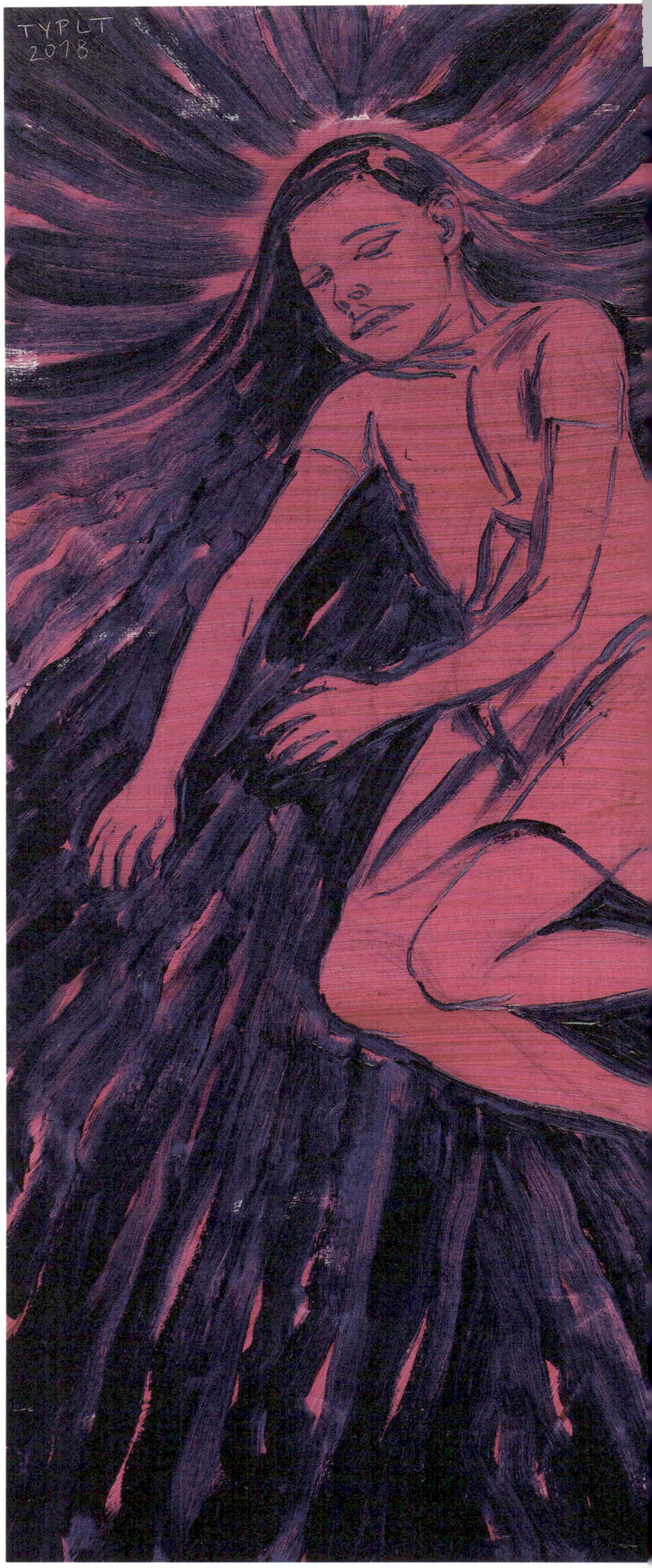
TYPLT
2018

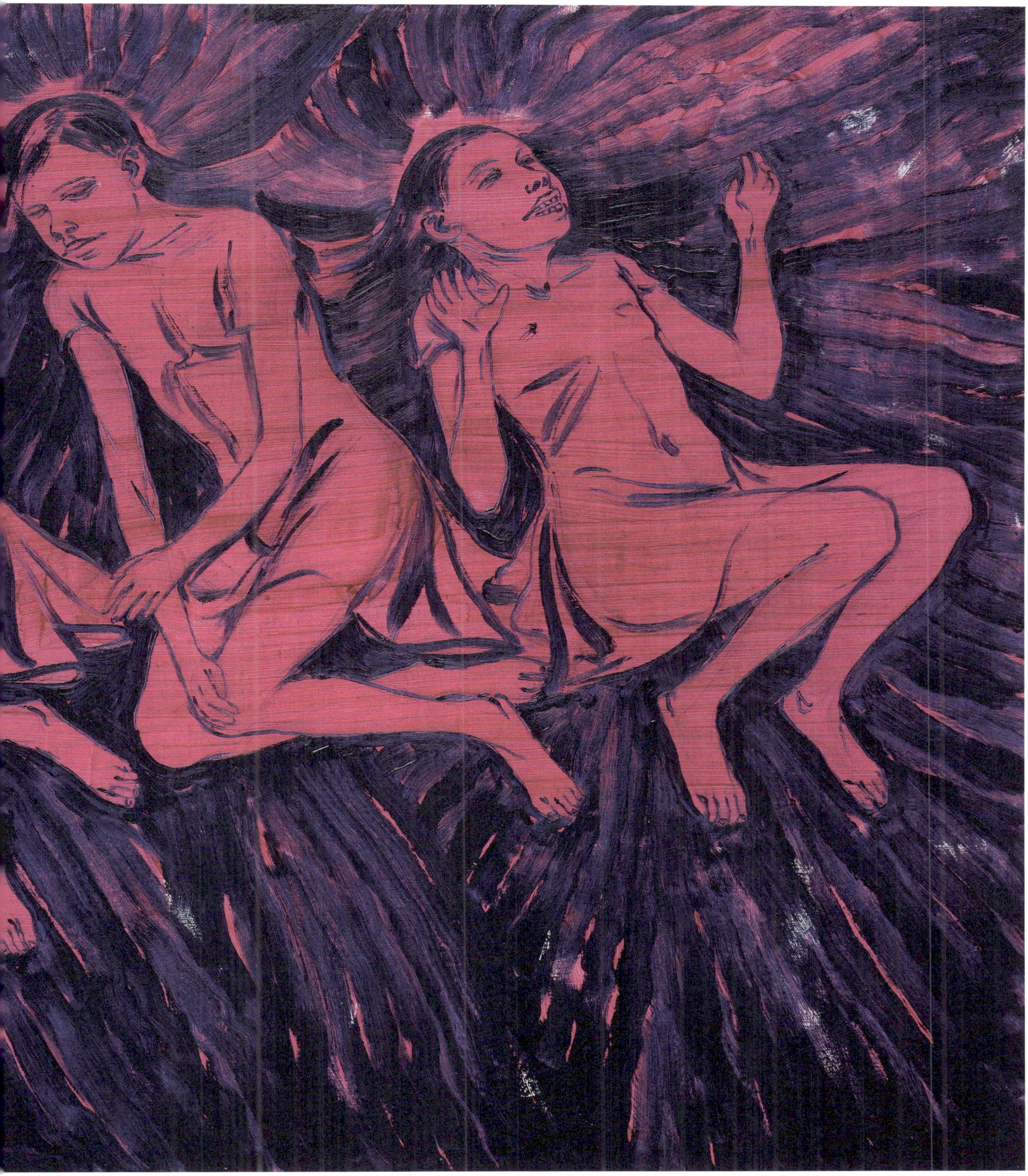

Phosphor / Phosphor
2018, Öl auf Leinwand, 200 × 260 cm

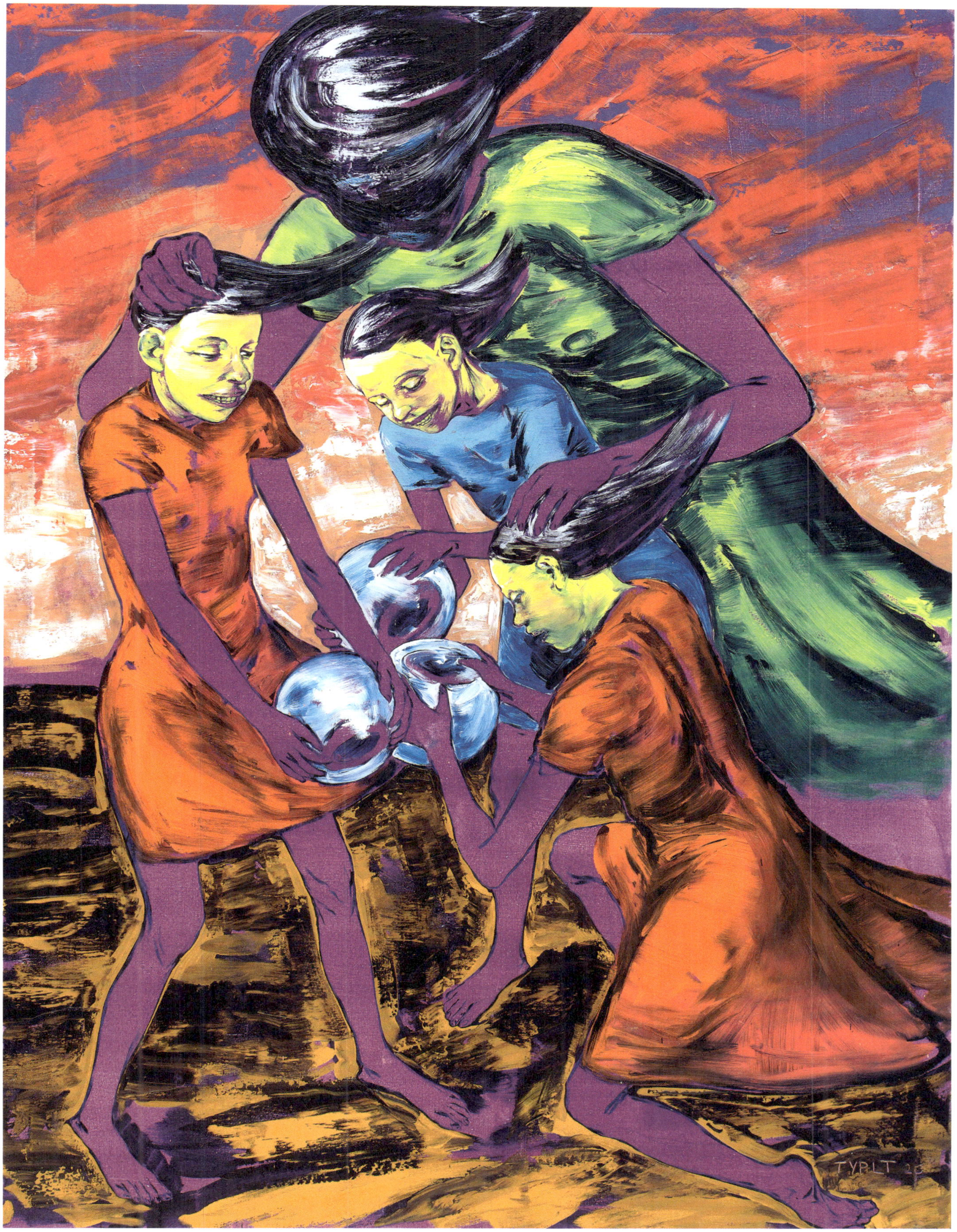

Irgendwie ein bisschen zu viel Ruhe hier / Somehow It's Too Quite Here
2020, Öl auf Leinwand, 240 × 180 cm

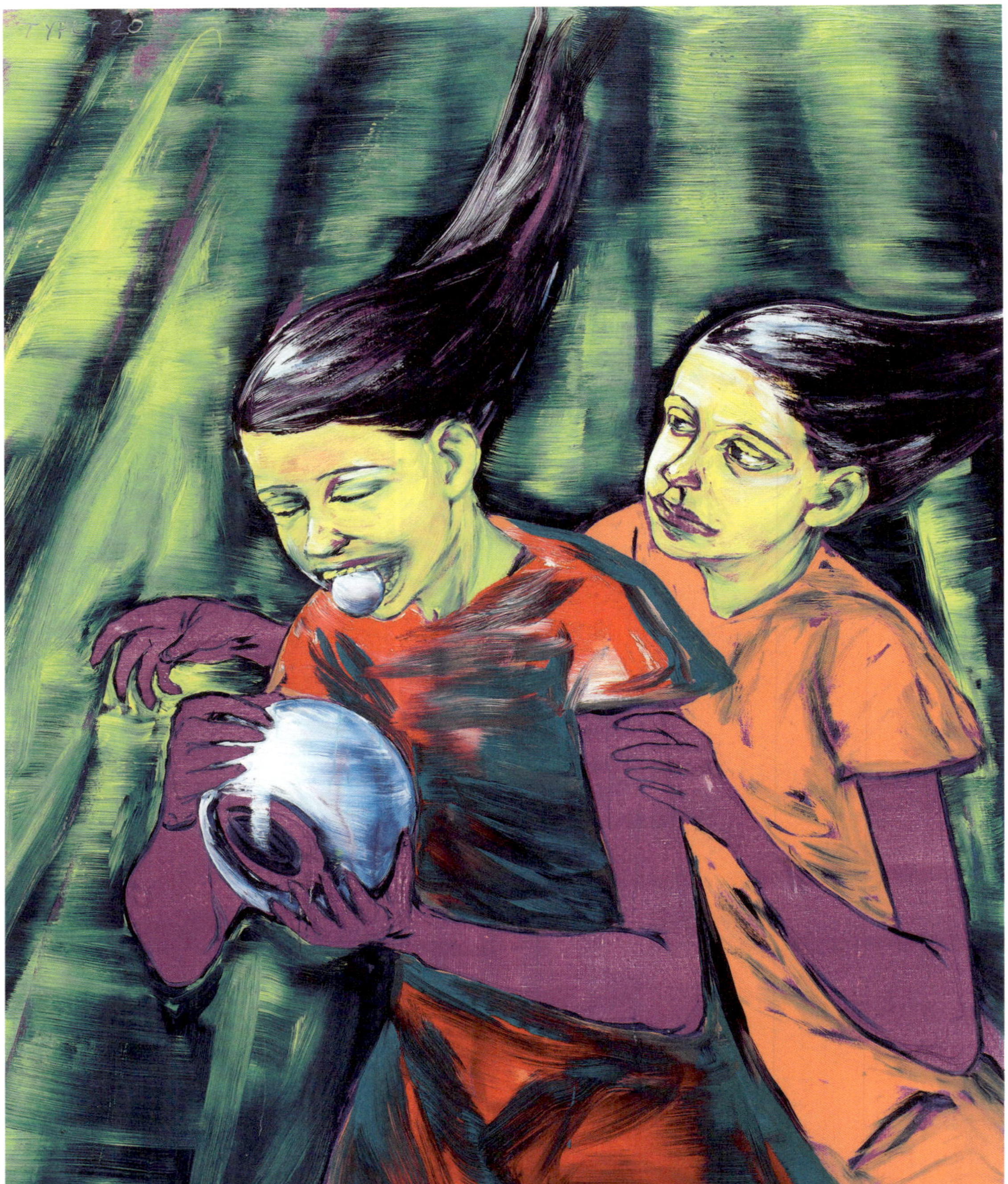

Schweigende / Silent Girl
2020, Öl auf Leinwand, 160 × 130 cm

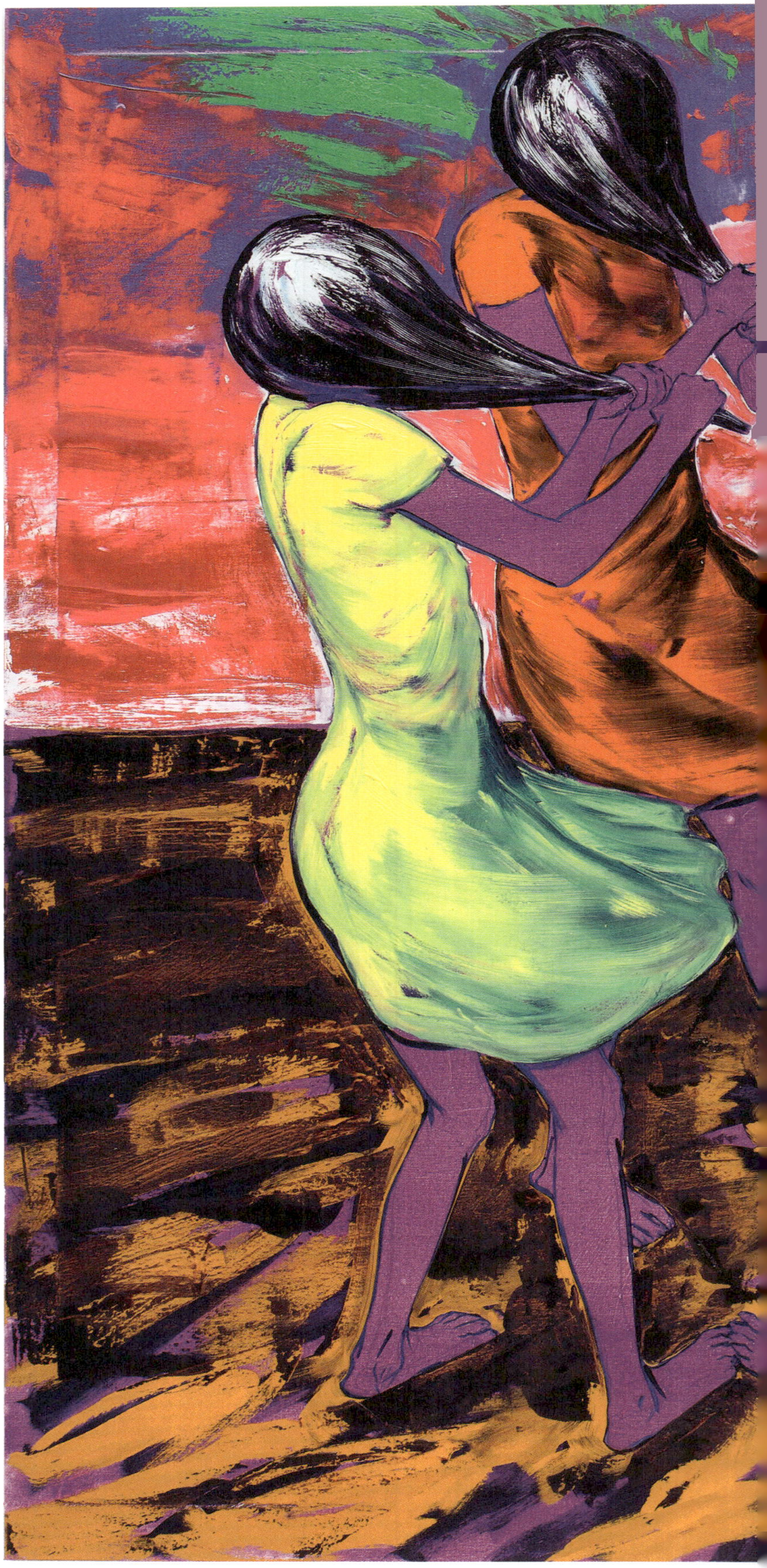

Pentagon / Pentagon
2020, Öl auf Leinwand, 200 × 260 cm

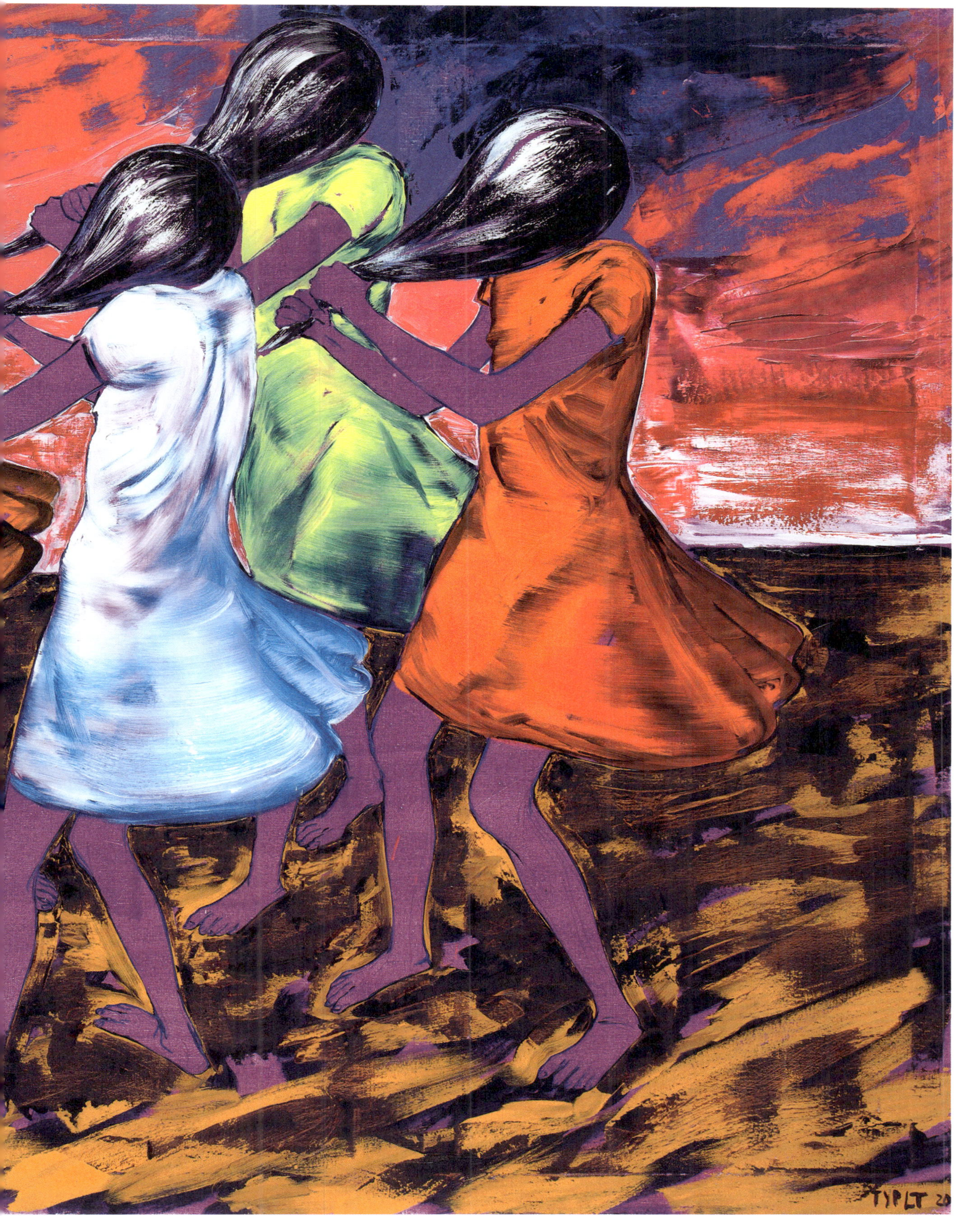

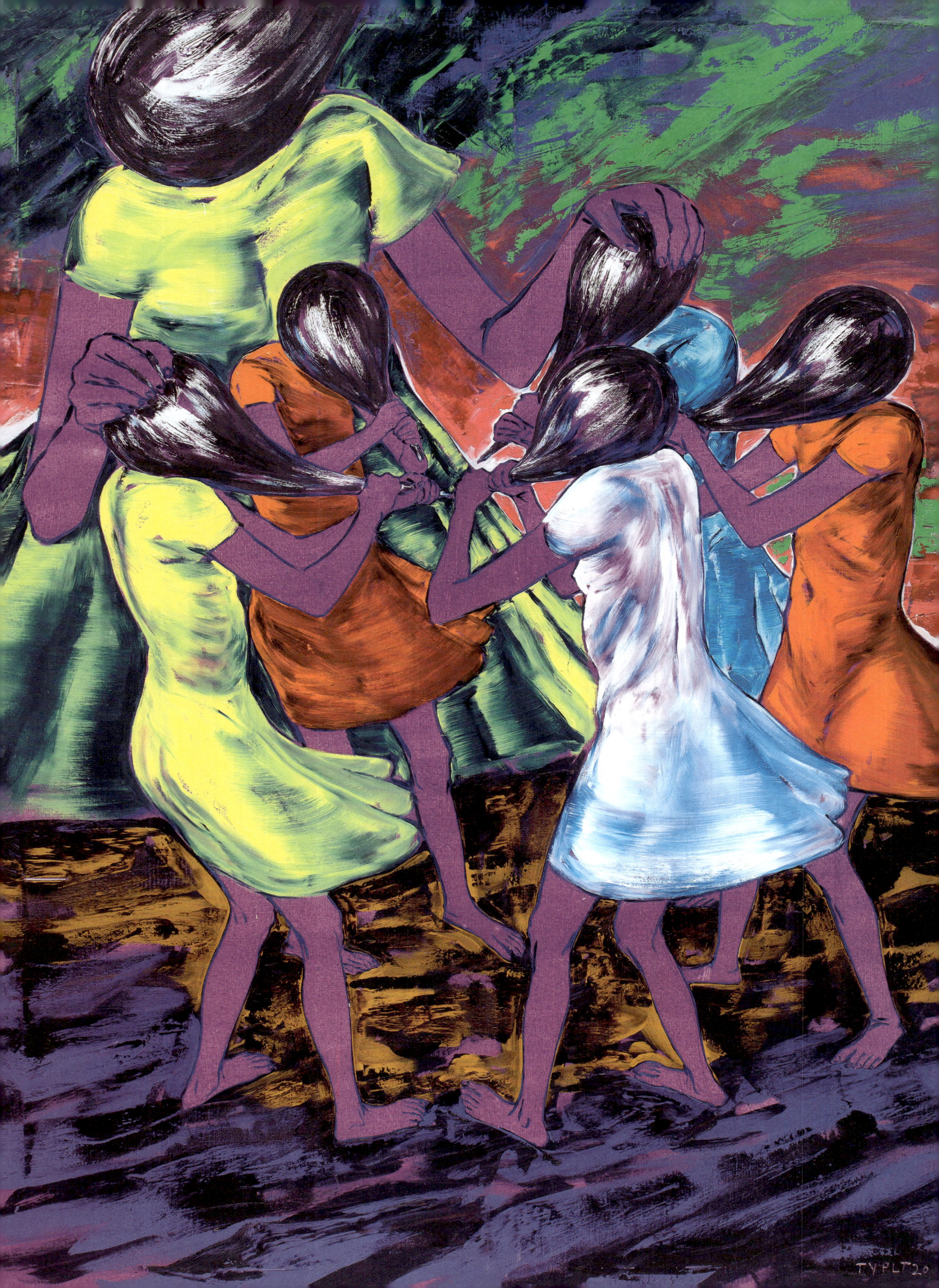

Tanzendes Pentagon / Dancing Pentagon
2020, Öl auf Leinwand, 260 × 200 cm

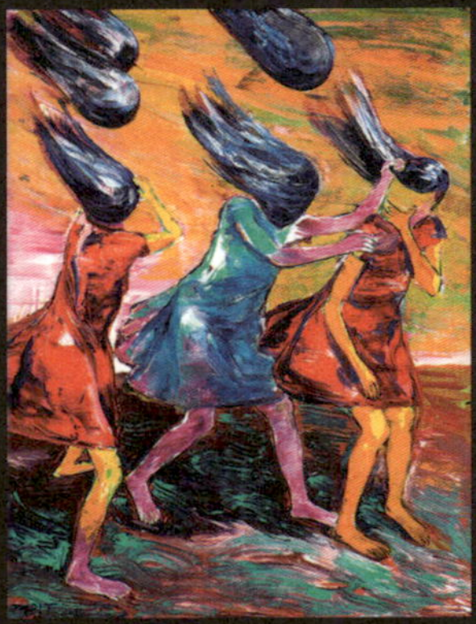

Zieh mir an den Haaren
Pull my Hair
2015, oil on canvas
240 × 180 cm
HoMA Collection, Nymburk

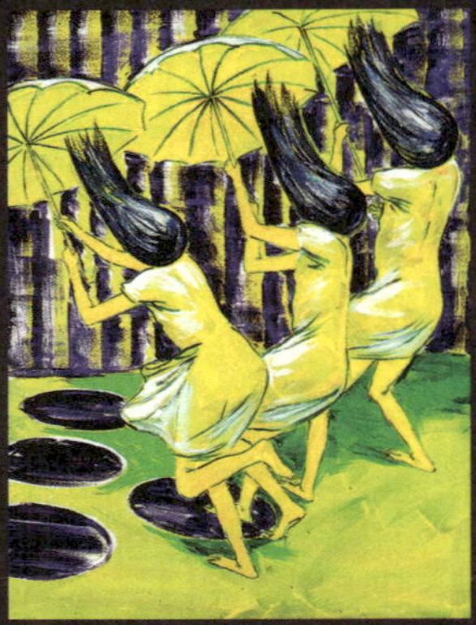

Japanerinnen im Wind
Japanese Women in the Wind
2019, oil on canvas
240 × 180 cm
COLLETT Prague | Munich

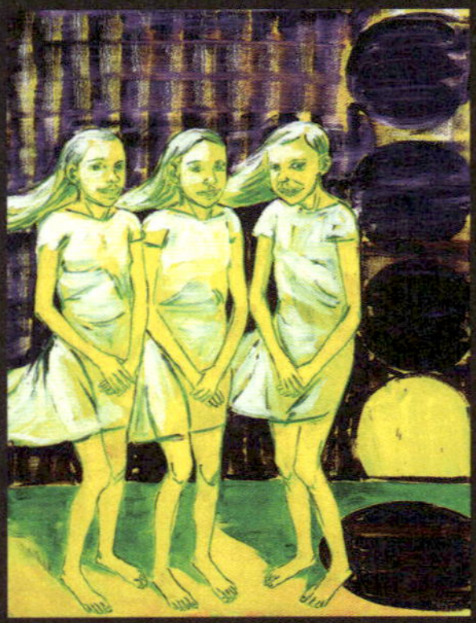

Violette Sonne
Purple Sun
2019, oil on canvas
240 × 180 cm
HoMA Collection, Nymburk

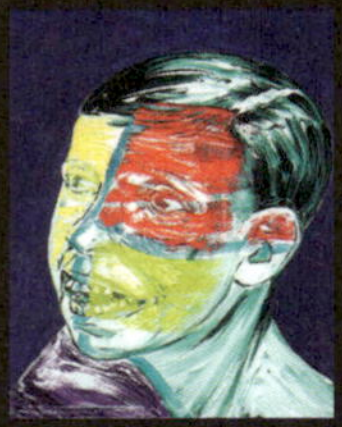

Illusionist
Illusionist
2020, oil on canvas
130 × 100 cm

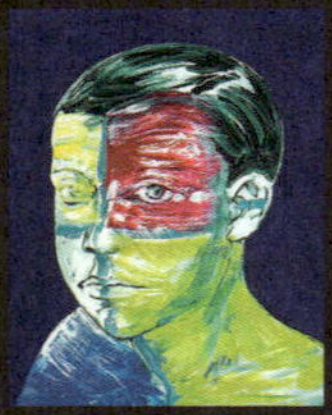

Hypnotiseur
Hypnotist
2020, oil on canvas
130 × 100 cm

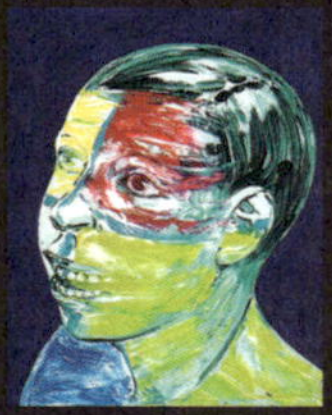

Mathematiker
Mathematician
2020, oil on canvas
130 × 100 cm

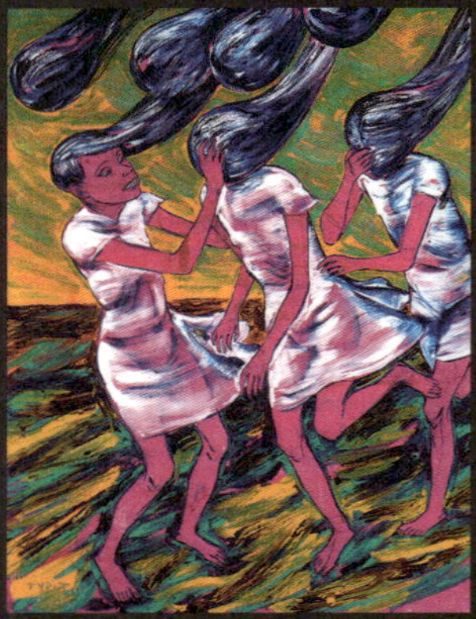

Somnambul
Somnambulistic
2019, oil on canvas
240 × 180 cm

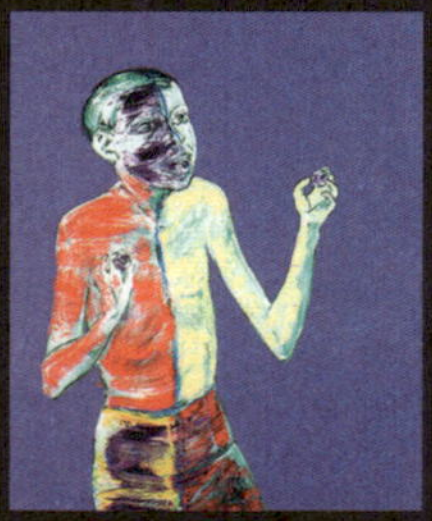

Einzelgänger in Violett,
Loner in Purple
2019, oil on canvas
160 × 130 cm
Private collection, Prague

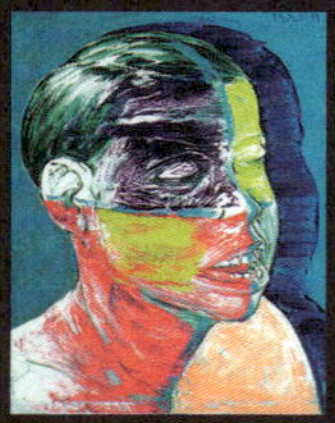

Konterrevolutionär
Counter-Revolutionary
2019, oil on canvas
130 × 100 cm
HoMA Collection, Nymburk

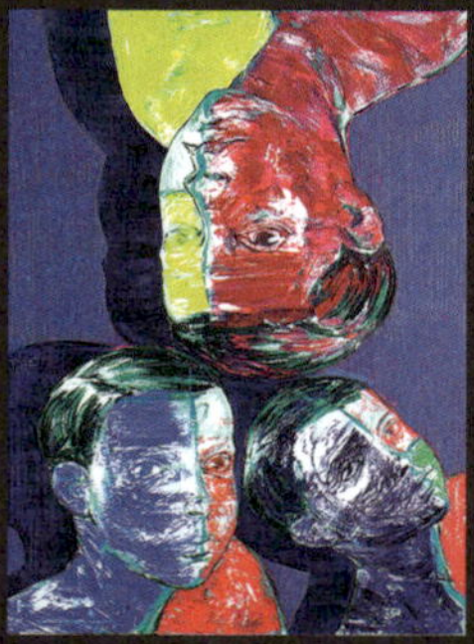

Astronauten
Astronauts
2019, oil on canvas
200 × 145 cm

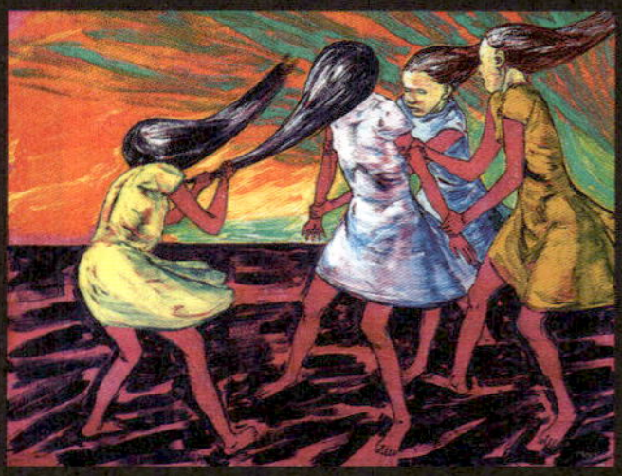

Fusion
Fusion
2020, oil on canvas
200 × 260 cm
Rosecky Collection

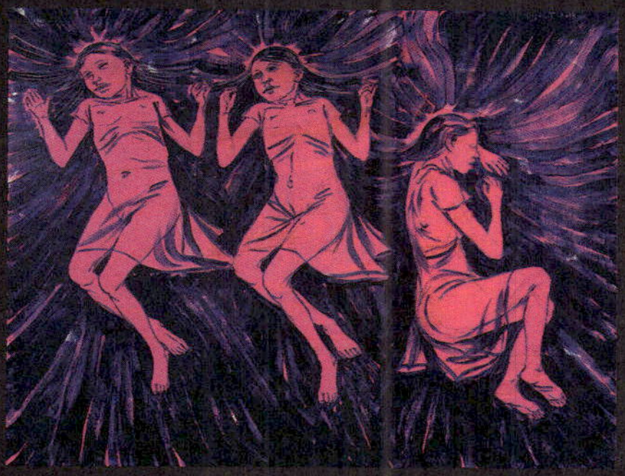

Sonne im Vollmond
Sun in the Full Moon
2018, oil on canvas
200 × 260 cm
HoMA Collection, Nymburk

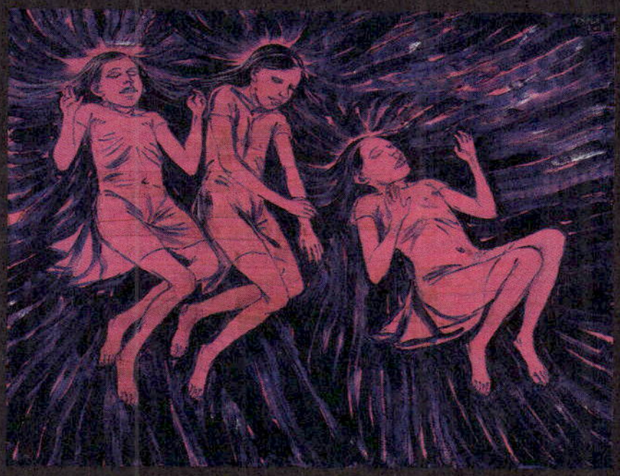

Bring mir das Phosphor aller Streichholzköpfe
Bring All the Match-Heads You Can Find
2018, oil on canvas
200 × 260 cm
Private collection, Nová Paka

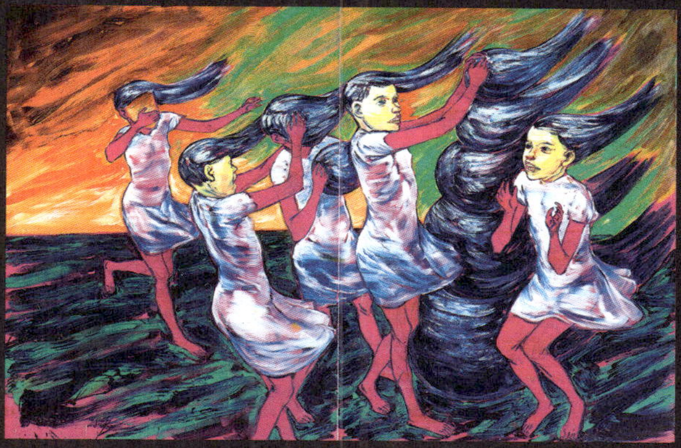

Der Wind wirft keinen Schatten
Wind Casts No Shadow
2020, oil on canvas
240 × 360 cm (two parts)

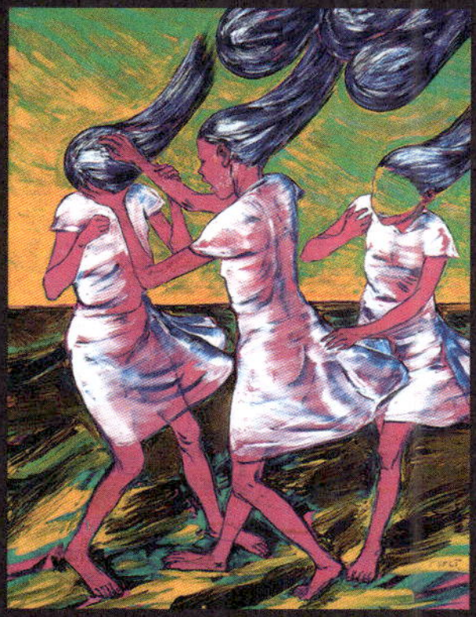

Sekundantinnen
Seconds to the Duel
2019, oil on canvas
240 × 180 cm

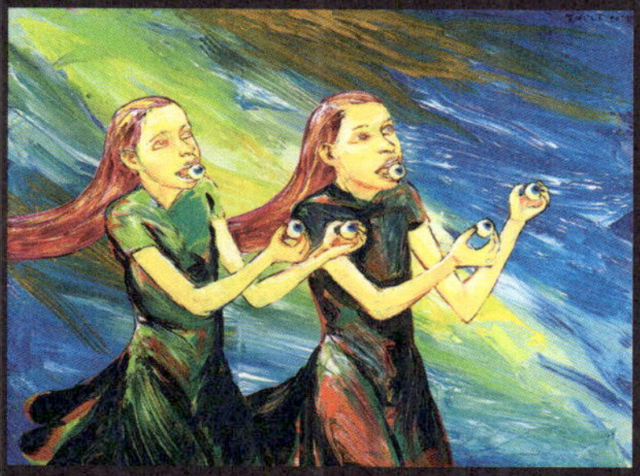

Einzelgängerinnen
Loners
2019, oil on canvas
180 × 240 cm
Private collection, Brno

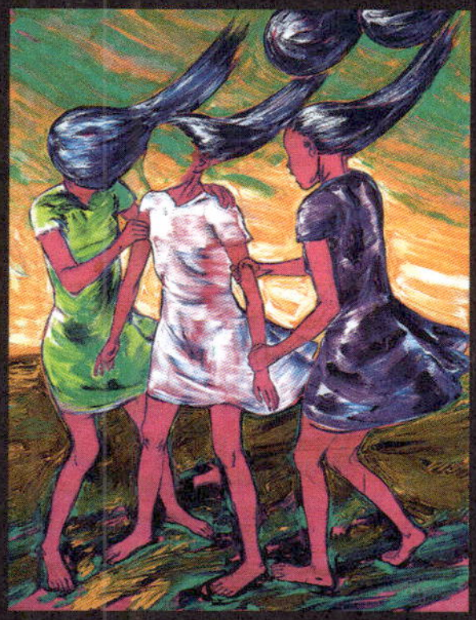

Abendstern
Evening Star
2019, oil on canvas
240 × 180 cm
Private collection, Roudnice nad Labem

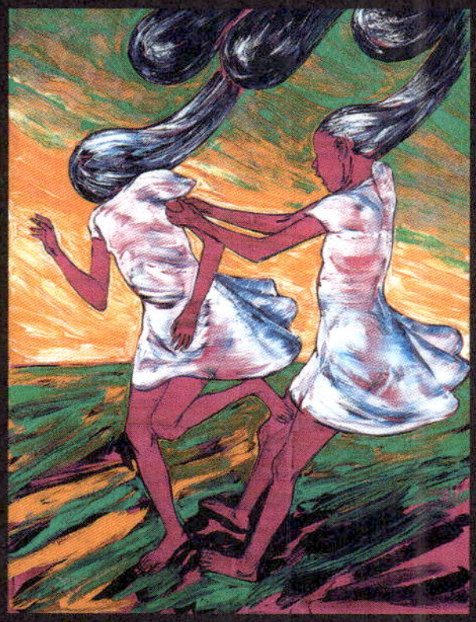

Duell
Duel
2019, oil on canvas
240 × 180 cm

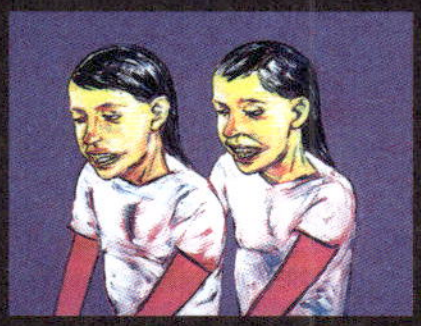

Violetter Dienstag
Purple Tuesday
2020, oil on canvas
100 × 130 cm

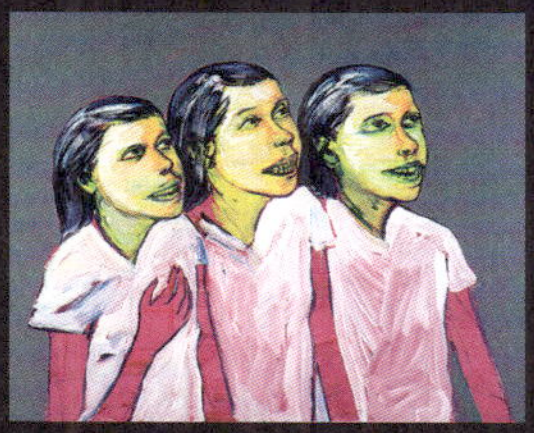

Bleierner Sonntag
Leaden Sunday
2019, oil on canvas
130 × 160 cm

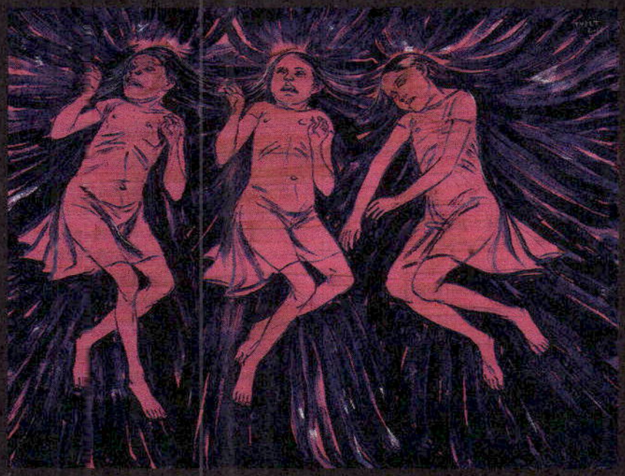

Ich würde der Sonne gern helfen zu brennen
I'd Like to Help the Sun to Shine
2018, oil on canvas
200 × 260
HoMA Collection, Nymburk

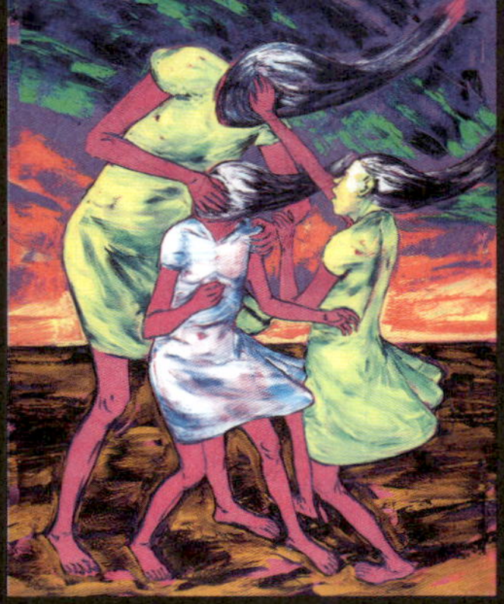

Die Himmelszangen schlossen sich
The Heavens Have Closed their Grip
2020, oil on canvas
260 × 200 cm

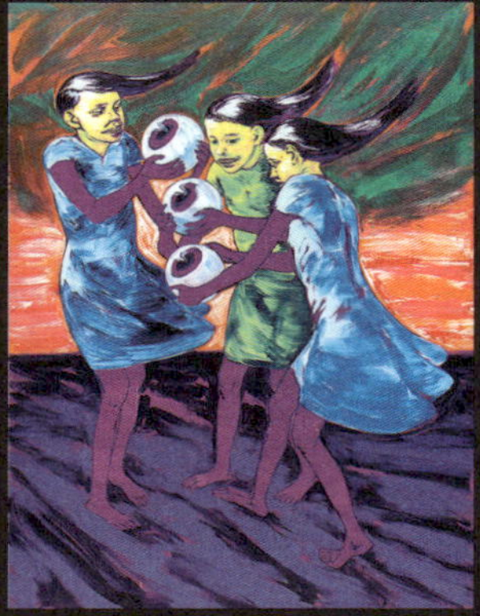

Um einen Schritt näher
One Step Closer
2020, oil on canvas
240 × 180 cm

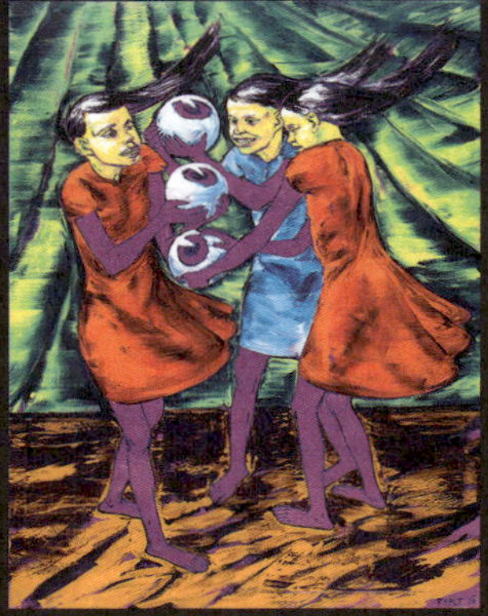

Spaltung
Split
2020, oil on canvas
240 × 180 cm

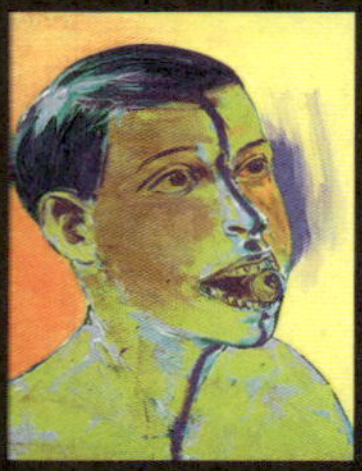

Violette Grenze
Purple Border
2019, oil on canvas
140 × 105 cm

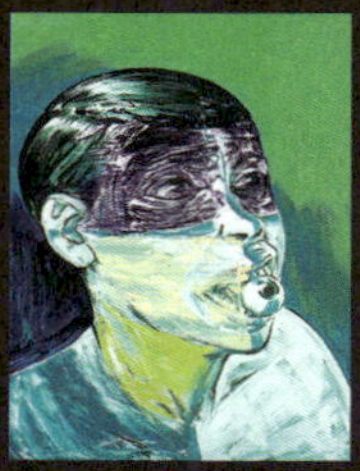

Violetter Hypnotiseur
Purple Hypnotist
2020, oil on canvas
140 × 105 cm

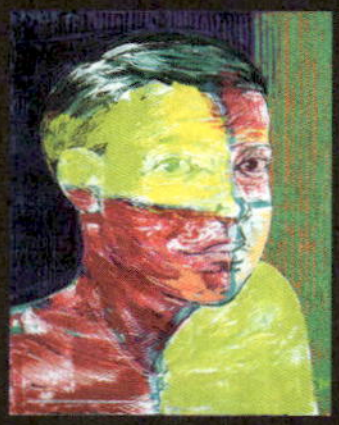

Pataphysiker
Pataphysicist
2019, oil on canvas
130 × 100 cm

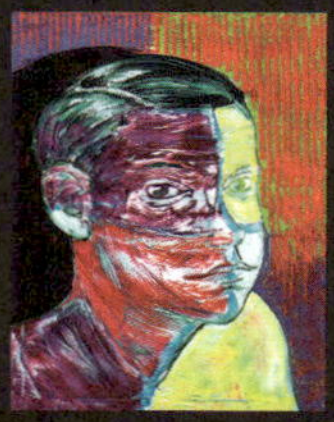

Erster Sekundant
Primary Second to the Duel
2020, oil on canvas
130 × 100 cm

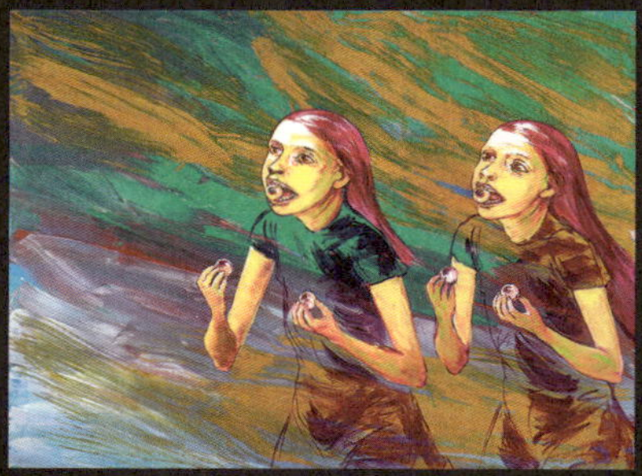

Mein Gesicht hat tausend Augen
My Face Has a Thousand Eyes
2020, oil on canvas
180 × 240 cm
Private collection, Kutná Hora

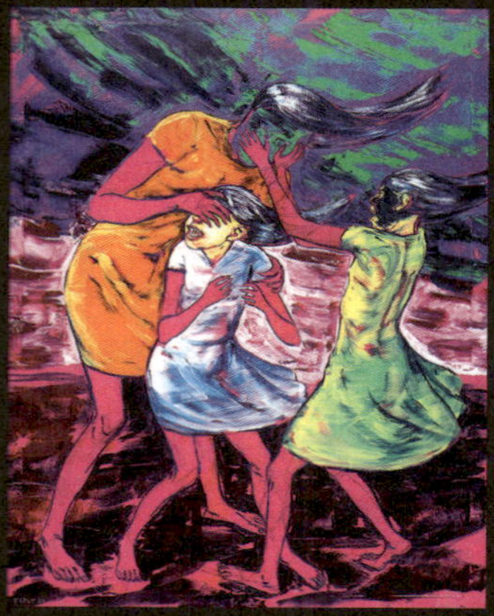

Nächtliche Fusion
Nocturnal Fusion
2020, oil on canvas
260 × 200 cm

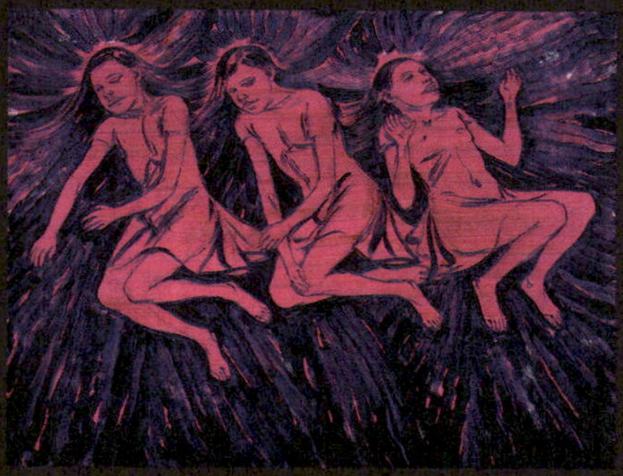

Phosphor
Phosphor
2018, oil on canvas
200 × 260 cm
HoMA Collection, Nymburk

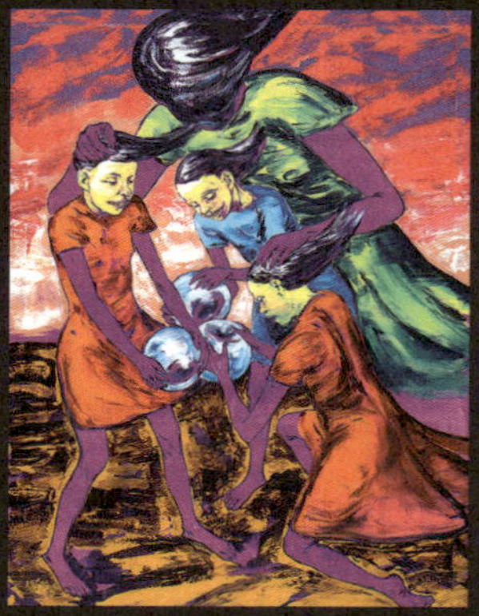

Irgendwie ein bisschen zu viel Ruhe hier
Somehow It's Too Quiet Here
2020, oil on canvas
240 × 180 cm

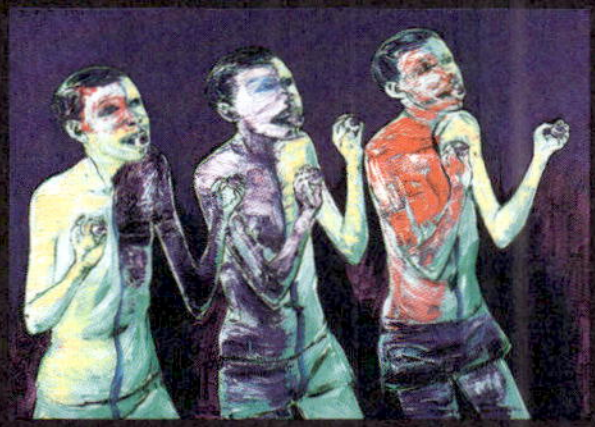

Zu Hause
At Home
2019, oil on canvas
145 × 200 cm

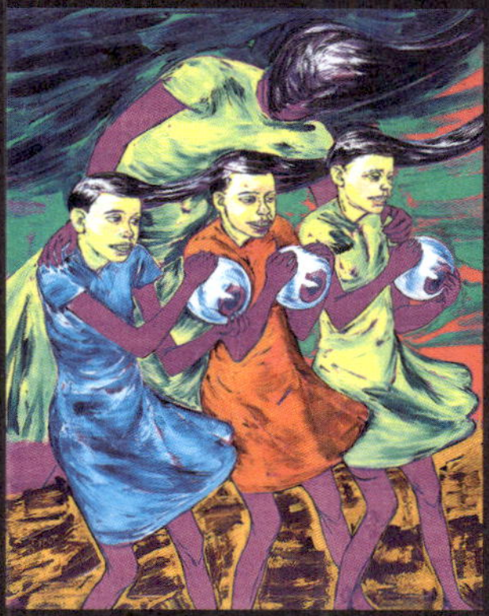

Die Zeit beugte sich im Bunde
Time Has Leant Forward
2020, oil on canvas
240 × 180 cm
Private collection, Prague

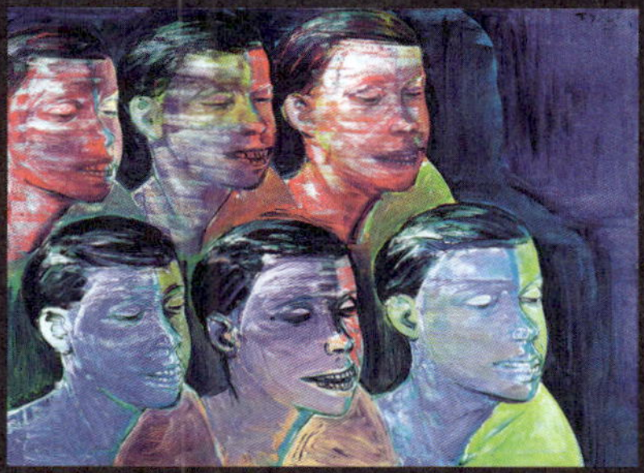

Patrioten
Patriots
2019, oil on canvas
180 × 240 cm
HoMA Collection, Nymburk

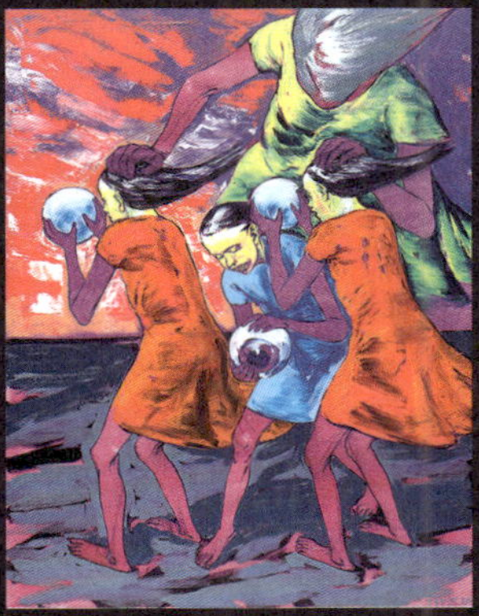

Beton
Concrete
2020, oil on canvas
240 × 180 cm
HoMA Collection, Nymburk

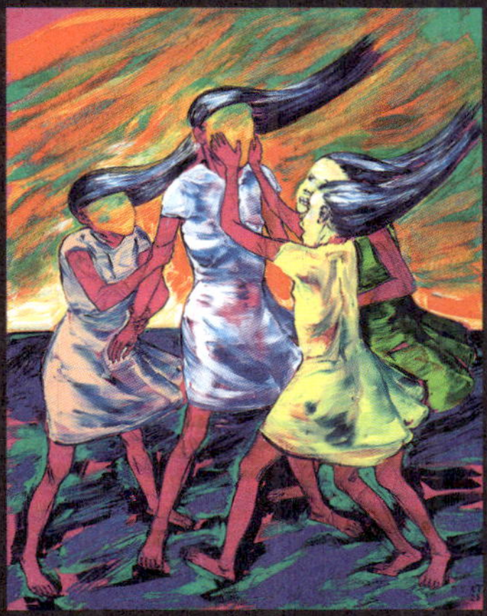

Vertikale Fusion
Vertical Fusion
2020, oil on canvas
260 × 200 cm
Private collection, Prague

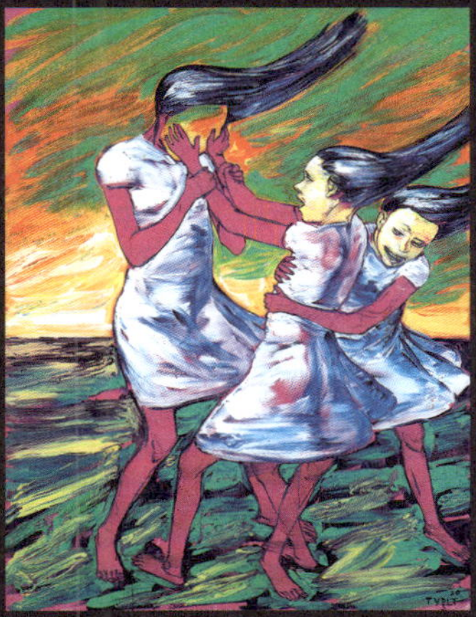

Große Fusion
Great Fusion
2020, oil on canvas
240 × 180 cm
COLLETT Prague I Munich

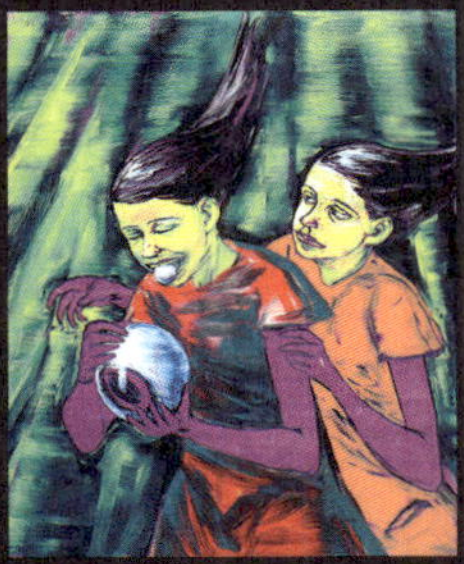

Schweigende
Silent Girl
2020, oil on canvas
160 × 130 cm

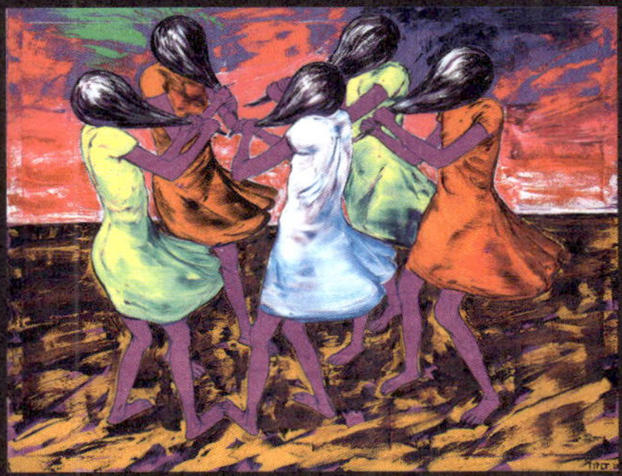

Pentagon
Pentagon
2020, oil on canvas
200 × 260 cm
Private collection, Prague

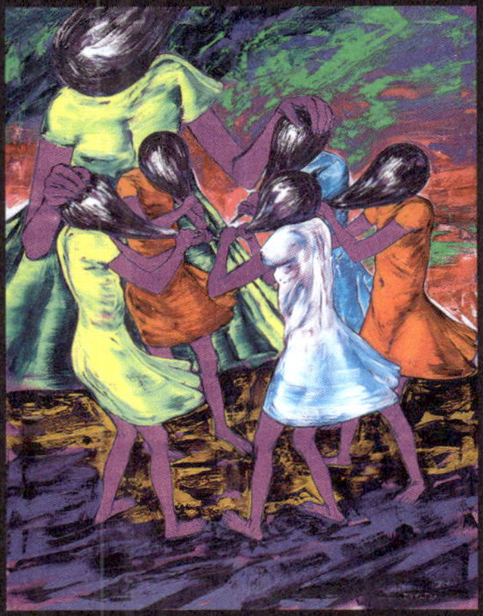

Tanzendes Pentagon
Dancing Pentagon
2020, oil on canvas
260 × 200 cm

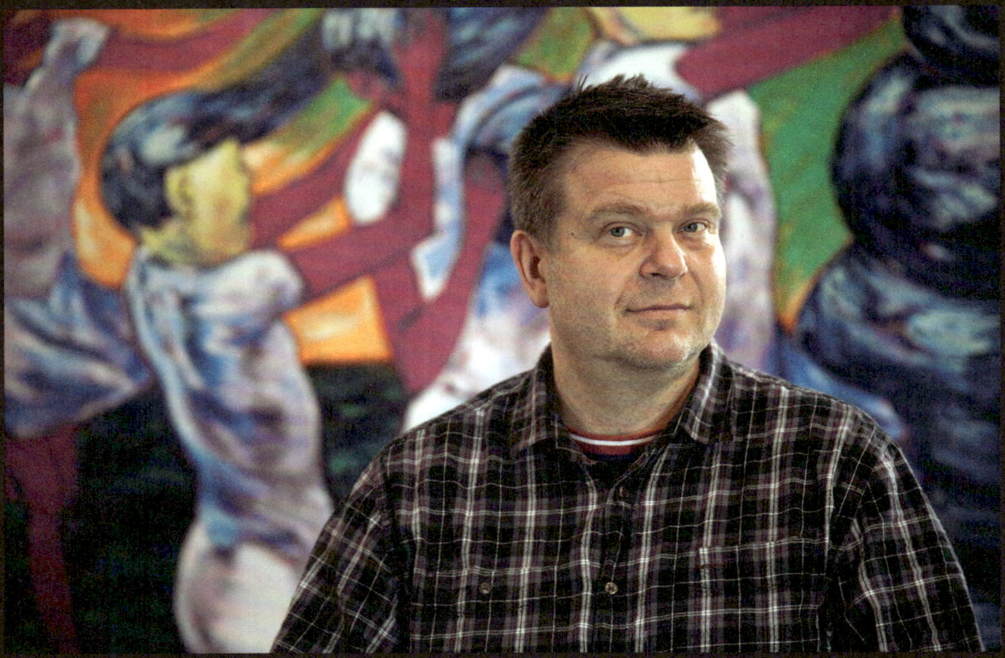

Lubomír Typlt

1975
Lubomír Typlt wird im nordböhmischen Nová Paka in Tschechien geboren

1989–1993
Besuch der Mittelschule für Gestaltung Václav Hollar in Prag

1993–1997
Beginn des Studiums an der Akademie für Kunst, Architektur und Design in Prag (UMPRUM) bei Prof. Jiří Šalamoun im Fach Illustration

1997–2001
Erstes Malereistudium an der Fakultät der Bildenden Künste im mährischen Brno (dt. Brünn) bei Prof. Jiří Načeradský

1998–2000
Zweites Malereistudium an der Kunstakademie Düsseldorf in der Klasse von Prof. Markus Lüpertz

2000–2002
Fortsetzung des Studiums der Malerei an der Kunstakademie Düsseldorf bei Prof. Gerhard Merz

2002–2005
Fortsetzung des Studiums der Malerei an der Kunstakademie Düsseldorf mit Wechsel in die Klasse von Prof. A. R. Penck

2004
Abschluss des Studiums an der Kunstakademie Düsseldorf als Meisterschüler von Prof. A. R. Penck

2005
Erhalt des Akademiebriefs der Kunstakademie Düsseldorf

2005–2011
Lubomír Typlt lebt und arbeitet in Berlin und Prag

Seit 2011 entstehen Lubomír Typlts Bilder in seinem Atelier in Pičín etwa 40 Kilometer südwestlich von Prag

1975
Lubomír Typlt is born in the North Bohemian town of Nová Paka

1989–1993
Attends the Václav Hollar Secondary School of Art in Prague

1993–1997
Studies illustration under Prof. Jiří Šalamoun at the Academy of Art, Architecture and Design in Prague (UMPRUM)

1997–2001
Studies painting under Prof. Jiří Načeradský at Brno University of Technology’s Faculty of Fine Arts

1998–2000
Studies painting under Prof. Markus Lüpertz at the Kunstakademie Düsseldorf

2000–2002
Continues his study of painting at the Kunstakademie Düsseldorf under Prof. Gerhard Merz

2002–2005
Switches to the Kunstakademie Düsseldorf’s painting course led by Prof. A. R. Penck

2004
Completes his studies at the Kunstakademie Düsseldorf as a *Meisterschüler* (master student) of Prof. A. R. Penck

2005
Receives his *Akademiebrief* (academic letter) from the Kunstakademie Düsseldorf

2005–2011
Lubomír Typlt lives and works in Berlin and Prague

Since 2011, Lubomír Typlt has been creating his paintings in his studio in Pičín, located roughly forty kilometres south-west of Prague

Einzel- und Gruppenausstellungen (Auswahl)

2001
Einzelausstellung in der Prager Galerie Václav Špála. Anfang der Zusammenarbeit mit privaten Galerien in Deuschland und Tschechien.

2006
Ausstellung *Das Recht auf Unreife* zusammen mit vier weiteren Absolventen der Klasse A. R. Penck in der Galerie Michael Schultz in Berlin.

Einzelausstellung *Die Unendlichkeit beschleunigen* in der Galerie der Hauptstadt Prag.

2007
Gruppenausstellung *Resetting. Verschiedene Wege zur Sachlichkeit* in der Galerie der Hauptstadt Prag.

2009
Einzelausstellung *Nur ein Ausländer kann so lachen* in der Galerie Ars in Brno.

2010
Ausstellung *Ich Typlt, Du Typlt* in der Galerie Zdeněk Sklenář in Prag.

2011
Parallel zur Einzelausstellung *Mythos und Metamorphose* von Markus Lüpertz, der zum ersten Mal in seiner nordböhmischen Geburtsstadt Liberec (dt. Reichenberg) ausstellt, findet in der Staatlichen Galerie der Region Liberec Lubomír Typlts Ausstellung *Wer wohnt in den Herzkammern?* mit einer Auswahl von Arbeiten auf Papier statt.

Einzelausstellung *Mobilisation* im Haus der Herren von Kunštát in Brno.

Ausstellung *Markus Lüpertz, A. R. Penck und ihr Schüler Lubomír Typlt* in der Galerie Zdeněk Sklenář in Prag, an dessen Entstehung sich der Galerist Michael Werner beteiligt.

2012
Einzelausstellung *Der Tickende Mann* in der Galerie der Hauptstadt Prag.

2013
Gruppenausstellung *Schmetterlingseffekt?* in der Prager Galerie Rudolfinum.

Ausstellung *Dunkel ist die Nacht* in der Galerie Poll in Berlin.

2014
Ausstellung *Großes Konsilium* in der Galerie Ars in Brno.

Ausstellung *A. R. Penck – Lubomír Typlt '19(75)'* in der C&K Galerie in Berlin.

2015
Ausstellung *Penck – Typlt* im Haus Topič in Prag.

Veröffentlichung der Monografie *The Ticking Man*, in der der tschechische Kunstwissenschaftler Karel Srp die Entwicklung von Lubomír Typlts Arbeit seit 1996 beschreibt. Die Monografie enthält zahlreiche Abbildungen der bis dato wichtigsten Werke.

2016
Ausstellung *Junge Götter* in der Galerie Zdeněk Sklenář in Prag.

Einzelausstellung *Transition* in der Pariser Galerie Oneiro und *Ticking Man* im Centre tchèque de Paris.

2017
In Brüssel zeigt die Vertretung der Hauptstadt Prag, das Prague House, die Ausstellung *Ticking Man*.

Einzelausstellung *370° des Kreises* in der DSC Gallery in Prag sowie Folgeausstellung *Visionäre* mit Papierarbeiten in der Galerie U Betlémské kaple in Prag.

2018
Die Staatliche Galerie der Region Hochland in Jihlava [dt. Iglau] zeigt Typlts Einzelausstellung *Die Maisesser*.

Einzelausstellung in der Galerie Václav Špála unter dem *Titel Man ertrinkt nicht zweimal in demselben Fluss*.

2019
Doppelausstellung *Příčný řez / A Cross-Section* von Jiří Načeradský und Lubomír Typlt in der Galerie der Modernen Kunst in Hradec Králové (dt. Königgrätz).

Gruppenausstellungen *Blue Is Hot and Red Is Cold* in Düsseldorf (Kulturbahnhof Eller und Kunsthalle Düsseldorf) und *Die haben einen Vogel* in der C&K Galerie in Berlin.

2020
Einzelausstellung Somnambul in der C&K Galerie in Berlin.

Sammlungen

Lubomír Typlt ist vertreten in zahlreichen privaten Sammlungen in Tschechien, der Slowakei, Deutschland, der Schweiz, den Niederlanden und Katar, u. a. in den Sammlungen folgender Museen, Galerien und Mäzene:

CZ
Museum der Modernen Kunst Olomouc
Regionalgalerie Liberec
Kunsthalle Praha
Galerie Klatovy – Klenová, Klatovy
Galerie für moderne Kunst in Hradec Králové
COLLETT Prague | Munich
Sammlung Robert Runták, Olomouc
Sammlung HoMA, Nymburk
SbírKa, Prag
Sammlung Kolowrat-Krakowský, Prag
Sammlung Richard Adam, Brno

NL
The Sublime Hyacinth Collection

CN
Sammlung Jidi Majia, Sichuan

Solo and group exhibitions (selection)

2001
Solo exhibition at Prague's Václav Špála Gallery. First collaboration with private galleries in Germany and the Czech Republic.

2006
The Right to Immaturity, group exhibition with four other graduates of A. R. Penck's painting course at the Michael Schultz Gallery in Berlin.

Accelerate Infinity, solo exhibition at Prague City Gallery.

2007
Resetting: Alternative Ways to Objectivity, group exhibition at Prague City Gallery.

2009
Only a Foreigner Could Laugh Like That, solo exhibition at Ars Gallery, Brno.

2010
I Typlt You Typlt at the Zdeněk Sklenář Gallery in Prague.

2011
In conjunction with the solo exhibition *Myth and Metamorphosis* by Markus Lüpertz – his first exhibition in his place of birth, the north Bohemian town of Liberec (German: Reichenberg) – the Liberec Regional Art Gallery hosts Lubomír Typlt's exhibition of selected works on paper, *Who Lives in the Chambers of the Heart?*

Mobilisation, solo exhibition at the House of the Lords of Kunštát, Brno.

Markus Lüpertz, A. R. Penck, and their Student Lubomír Typlt at the Zdeněk Sklenář Gallery in Prague, co-organized by the gallerist Michael Werner.

2012
The Ticking Man, solo exhibition at Prague City Gallery.

2013
The Butterfly Effect?, group exhibition at Galerie Rudolfinum, Prague.

Dark Is the Night at Galerie Poll in Berlin.

2014
The Great Council at Ars Gallery, Brno.

A. R. Penck – Lubomír Typlt '19(75)' at C&K Galerie in Berlin.

2015
Penck – Typlt at the Topič Salon in Prague.

Publication of the monograph *The Ticking Man*, in which the Czech art historian Karel Srp describes the evolution of Typlt's art since 1996. The book contains numerous reproductions of his most important works to date.

2016
Young Gods at the Zdeněk Sklenář Gallery.

Two solo exhibitions in Paris: *Transition* at Galerie Oneiro and *The Ticking Man* at the Czech Center.

2017
Prague's official representation in Brussels, the Prague House, shows *The Ticking Man.*

370° of the Circle, solo exhibition at DSC Gallery in Prague, followed by *Visionaries*, an exhibition of works on paper at the Bethlehem Chapel Gallery in Prague.

2018
The Vysočina Regional Gallery in Jihlava presents Typlt's solo exhibition *The Corn Eaters.*

You Can't Drown in the Same River Twice, solo exhibition at the Václav Špála Gallery.

2019
Double exhibition *Příčný řez / A Cross-Section* by Jiří Načeradský and Lubomír Typlt at the Gallery of Modern Art in Hradec Králové.

Two group exhibitions in Germany: *Blue Is Hot and Red Is Cold* in Düsseldorf (Kulturbahnhof Eller and Kunsthalle Düsseldorf) and *For Birds' Sake* at C&K Galerie in Berlin.

2020
Solo exhibition *Somnambul* at C&K Galerie in Berlin.

Collections

Lubomír Typlt is represented in numerous private collections in the Czech Republic, Slovakia, Germany, Switzerland, the Netherlands and Qatar, including the collections of the following museums, galleries and patrons:

CZ
Olomouc Museum of Art
Liberec Regional Art Gallery
Kunsthalle Praha
Klatovy – Klenová Gallery, Klatovy
Gallery of Modern Art in Hradec Králové
COLLETT Prague | Munich
Robert Runták Collection, Olomouc
HoMA Collection, Nymburk
SbírKa, Prague
Kolowrat-Krakowský Collection, Prague
Richard Adam Collection, Brno

NL
The Sublime Hyacinth Collection

CN
Jidi Majia Collection, Sichuan

This publication is released to accompany the exhibition
Diese Publikation erscheint anlässlich der Ausstellung

Somnambul, 2020, C&K Galerie in Berlin

Editor / Herausgeber:
Christiane Bühling-Schultz

Editorial staff / Redaktion:
Lena Beleke

Design / Gestaltung:
Filip Kopecký

Photography / Fotografie:
Tomáš Souček, Lena Beleke

Image editing / Bildbearbeitung:
Radek Typovský

Copyediting / Lektorat:
Eva Hrubá, Lena Beleke, Wendy Brouwer, Susann Harring

Translations / Übersetzung:
Patrick Kremer, Stephan von Pohl

Production / Herstellung, Kerber Verlag:
Jens Bartneck

Project management / Projektmanagement, Kerber Verlag:
Martina Kupiak

Printed and published by / Gesamtherstellung:
Kerber Verlag
Windelsbleicher Str. 166–170
33659 Bielefeld
Germany
+49 521 95008-10
+49 521 95008-88 (F)
info@kerberverlag.com
kerberverlag.com

Kerber publications are distributed worldwide / Kerber Publikationen werden weltweit vertrieben:

ACC Art Books
Sandy Lane
Old Martlesham
Woodbridge, IP12 4SD
UK
+44 1394 38 99 50
+44 1394 38 99 99 (F)
accartbooks.com

Artbook | D.A.P.
75 Broad Street, Suite 630
New York, NY 10004
USA
+1 212 627 19 99
+1 212 627 94 84 (F)
artbook.com

AVA Verlagsauslieferung
Scheidegger
Obere Bahnhofstr. 10A
8910 Affoltern am Albis
Switzerland
+41 44 762 42 41
+41 44 762 42 49 (F)
avainfo@ava.ch

KNV Zeitfracht
Verlagsauslieferung
kerber-verlag@knv-zeitfracht.de

The Deutsche Nationalbibliothek lists this publication in the Deutsche Nationalbibliografie: dnb.de.
Die Deutsche Nationalbibliothek verzeichnet diese Publikation in der Deutschen Nationalbibliografie: dnb.de.

ISBN 978-3-7356-0747-8
www.kerberverlag.com

Printed in Germany